YOU CAN

NEVER GO WRONG

BY

BEING KIND

INSPIRING STORIES OF

KINDNESS & GENEROSITY

DR. ZEAL OKOGERI

YOU CAN

NEVER GO WRONG

BY

BEING KIND

INSPIRING STORIES OF
KINDNESS & GENEROSITY

Kindness Books
Honolulu, Hawaii

Published by Kindness Books

Honolulu, Hawaii

www.KindnessBooks.com

Library of Congress Control Number: 2020932113

ISBN: 9798605897385

First Printing: July 2017

Second Edition: February 2020

Revision: November 2020

Printed in the United States of America

CONTENTS

ACKNOWLEDGMENTS

I want to express my gratitude to the kind people who helped me in the course of creating the second edition of this book. Thank you to the story contributors, who unconditionally devoted their time and thoughts to compose their personal stories. I didn't have to convince them about the merit of being a vital part of this book. They intrinsically embraced the beautiful humanitarian concept of this book and wanted very much to be a part of it. Thank you to those who offered suggestions, provided encouragement and feedback; and Thank you to those who assisted in editing, proofreading, and designing the interior and cover of this book.

INTRODUCTION

Someone once asked me, "On all the subjects you can write and talk about, why kindness?"

To answer this question, let me tell you a story:

A wise man was nearing the end of his life and was surrounded by his disciples. He closed his eyes peacefully and grew silent, and his disciples thought he was gone. Escorted by an angel, he was transported to another realm, a realm of magnificent lights of unparalleled brilliance and a mesmerizing array of celestial sounds. But soon, he was back in his body, alert as ever, and whispers to his astonished disciples, "I have seen the other side."

"The other side?" Asked one of his disciples, as they all turned and looked at each other, bewildered.

"Heaven, and hell. I have seen them both."

The wise man continued, "I came upon a door, and behind it was hell. I was stunned by what I saw there. There was a dining hall filled with rows of tables, each table full of delicious food, yet the people seated around the tables were miserable and malnourished, moaning with hunger."

"As I came closer, I noticed that each person was holding a very long spoon, and their elbows strapped in a way that kept their arms extended. In this position, the poor souls were unable to bend the spoons to their mouths. Despite the abundance of food before them, they were starving."

He continued, "I left this horrible place and opened another door, one that led to heaven. Inside, I was surprised to see that very same scene before my eyes, a dining hall filled with row upon row of tables, each table full of delicious food. But instead of moaning with hunger, the people around the tables were well nourished and plump, sitting contentedly, talking and laughing with one another, satisfied with the abundance of food before them."

"I couldn't understand," said the wise man.
Then my angel explained it to me: "It is quite simple. Love requires demonstration. Unlike the people in hell, these people learned early on to share and take care of each other."

"I want you to pay close attention to what they are doing," said the angel.

"Indeed, as I observed, I noticed that, like those in hell, these people were holding the very same long spoons, and their elbows strapped in a way that kept their arms extended. But as I watched, a man dipped his spoon into a dish before him, but rather than struggling to feed himself, he extended his spoon and fed the woman seated across from him. This woman, filled with gratitude, returned the favor. She leaned across the table and fed the man."

"I suddenly understood the difference between heaven and hell," the wise man explained to his disciples. "It is neither the attributes of the place, nor its plentiful resources, but the way people treat each other."

There you have it. Simply put, kindness makes life easier. The work I'm doing, through my writings, talks, and stories, is intended to inspire love, kindness, and compassion. If kindness is universally accepted and applied, everyone would benefit.

Dr. Zeal Okogeri

Chapter One

THE GIFT OF LOVE

No act of kindness,
no matter how small, is ever wasted.

—Aesop

1

Kindness Soften Our Hearts

Sometimes we are the beneficiaries of kindness, and other times we are put in situations in which we can give the gift of kindness. A few years ago, I attended a spiritual seminar in Las Vegas. During the break, I boarded the bus at the intersection of Flamingo Road and Las Vegas Boulevard, near the Bellagio Hotel, to visit a friend. After visiting with my friend, I walked to the bus stop to catch a bus back to my hotel. A man was waiting for the bus, so I asked him when he expected the bus to arrive. "Probably in five minutes," he said.

Before long, we saw the bus approaching and people running toward us to board it. One of them was a big, rough-looking pony-tailed man with a super-sized Burger King drink in his hand. He rudely cut in front of everyone and started boarding the bus. But the driver stopped him, saying that drinks were not allowed aboard the bus. The man wouldn't hear of it. He started a nasty argument with the driver, trying to bully the driver into allowing him to keep the drink.

Meanwhile, the rest of us patiently lined up outside, waiting to board the bus. The gentleman with whom I had spoken earlier got fed up with the bully's behavior and said, "Look, it says up there on the sign that you cannot bring a drink inside the bus. Get rid of the damn drink, like the driver said, and get in." That did it! The bully angrily threw his drink out the door, barely missing us. He then verbally assaulted the man who had spoken up. Trying to move away from the escalating confrontation, we boarded the bus. The bully sat close to the driver. The gentleman who had spoken up sat in the back, and I sat in the middle of the bus. As the bus embarked on its route, the bully continued ranting at the man in the back of the bus. You could feel the tension crackling in the air. Passengers were sighing, mumbling, and rolling their eyes in disgust, but no one wanted to get directly involved.

I started chanting inwardly a mantra of love, compassion, and balance known as 'HU,' a love song to God and surrendering the situation to the Divine. My aim was to bring about harmony. When the bus approached the intersection of Las Vegas Boulevard and Flamingo Road, it was time for me to get off, Thank God! Interestingly, it was also the destination for the bully, as well as for the man whom he had been berating. Before the bus came to a stop, the bully, full of rage, walked toward the back of the bus for a face-to-face verbal confrontation. By this time, everyone's speculation of what was about to happen seemed imminent.

When the bus stopped, they got off, and I was directly behind them. As soon as we landed on the sidewalk, the bully confronted the other fellow, trying to elicit a response that could escalate into a fistfight. Without hesitation, I approached the bully. Looking directly into his eyes, I said:

"I'd like to buy you another drink."

He turned and glared down at me as if I were an ant.

"Excuse me?" He said in a deep voice.

"I noticed the bus driver made you throw out your drink, and I'd like to buy another drink for you," I elaborated.

As I spoke to him, the other fellow started walking away toward the Bellagio Hotel.

"Yeah, yeah, you can buy me another drink. It cost me $2. Figure you're trying to save your buddy over there," he said sarcastically.

"My buddy? Who?" I asked.

"Him over there, walking away. Hey, come back here," he screamed at the fellow.

"Leave him alone. I said I want to buy you another drink. I have no idea who the other guy is. We boarded the bus together," I explained.

At this point, the bully looked at me, bewildered. He couldn't believe I was trying to help a stranger in Las Vegas! As I reached in my pocket for money, I glanced at him. It was as though someone had poured hot water on an ice cube. He melted. He looked at me in my white African attire and seemed confused. In a humble and respectful tone, he said, "Sir, you keep your money; I'm all right."

"Life is tough enough as it is. There is no need to complicate it any further. We need to have peace," I explained.

He nodded his head in agreement, like a child being scolded by his mother. We shook hands. He thanked me for helping and explained that he was having a bad day. I acknowledged his situation by saying, "I understand," and thanked him wholeheartedly for cooperating. By the time our conversation concluded, the other man had disappeared into one of the hotels.

This is how a potentially violent confrontation was averted by the offer of love—a $2 drink. That's all it took to soften the bully's heart.

By Zeal Okogeri

2

The Man in the Yellow Raincoat

It was a cold and windy March afternoon. I was working a contract job in downtown Minneapolis and was coming back from my lunch break. I was already late at getting back. I was standing at a traffic light waiting to cross when I saw an older man crossing the street to my right and coming toward me. He stood out because he was wearing a bright yellow raincoat and a black fisherman's cap. In each hand, he carried a full shopping bag, and they looked quite heavy. He was struggling from their weight as he walked, and he was walking right into that stiff wind blowing down the street.

As I was watching him, suddenly, a heavy gust came up and blew the cap right off his head. A look of dismay quickly came to his face, and I knew he was trying to decide if he would try to fetch his cap or just let it go. He looked around, and we both saw his black hat swiftly tumbling down the street behind him. Then, with a weary shrug of his shoulders, he made his decision—he would let the cap go. He shuffled past me with a new layer of pain etched into his face. My heart went out to this man. I just stood there, even as the light changed so that I could cross. I thought, 'Should I go after his cap?' As I mentioned, I was already late from lunch, and our boss was not at all the forgiving type, …and what were the chances of even finding the cap?

So, I did what I often do when trying to make a decision in which I am pulled in two directions. I asked myself the question, "OK, tomorrow morning when I wake up and think back on today, will I regret not helping this man?"

I instantly knew that I would regret not at least trying to help. So, off I went down the street where I had last seen the cap tumbling away from us. Frankly, I didn't think I had a very good chance of finding it, as many minutes had passed since it had blown down the street.

But off I went. Even if I did find it, I wasn't sure I could find the old man again, since he might have gone down a side street as I was searching in the other direction. However, I was in luck. A couple of blocks down, some road construction was going on, and I found the cap stuck on metal fencing that was jutting into the street. Alright, now all I had to do was find the man!

I quickly ran back the other way, looking ahead for some yellow color amongst the throngs of people going here and there. But, alas, I couldn't see him anywhere. I ran some more blocks ahead, then resigned myself to the search. 'Oh well,' I thought, 'at least I tried.'

At the next corner, I came across a bench and thought that I would leave it there, and maybe, just maybe, he would pass by and see it.

Then, right as I went to lay it down, out of the corner of my eye, I caught a flash of yellow from inside a store across the street – and sure enough, it was him! He was picking up something at a tailor shop and, lucky for me, was standing right against the front window, his yellow raincoat in clear view.

My heart leaped with joy as I crossed the street and prepared to enter the store. As I went in, he had his back to me and was at the counter talking to the proprietor. I overheard him saying, "...and then, to make things even worse, this wind comes up and blows my cap right off my head! That was my favorite cap. I've had it for over 30 years, and now it's gone. I'm just so tired; I just didn't have the energy to go after it..." I saw the shop clerk look up at me as I came up behind the old man, lifting the cap and pointing at him, a big smile on my face. Then the shop clerk's face also broke into a wide grin, and he said, "Well, you know, sir, even after all that, I really do think this is your lucky day. Just turn around!"

The old man slowly turned around to face me, and I gently gave him back his treasured cap. To see the transformation on his face from pain to joy is something I'll never forget. I knew that I didn't have to say anything, and the old man himself said only two words: "Thank you, thank you!" I saw delight and joy fill his eyes, and deep gratitude was silently communicated to me with a slight nod of his head. I simply nodded back and then walked out of the store.

After that, I don't remember much of the walk back to work. Gone were the cold, the wind, my hurry, and my worry.

What was there instead was a depth of fulfillment in my heart that I feel to this day.

And sure enough, when I awoke the next morning and thought of the man in the yellow raincoat, a big smile came to my face. I thought about how close I had come to not helping; how close I had come to missing one of the most fulfilling experiences I have ever had in this life.

By John Villemonte

3

A Random Act of Roadside Assistance

During this past year, I've had three instances of car trouble. Each time one of these things happened, I was disgusted with the way most people hadn't bothered to help. One of those times, I was on the side of the road for close to three hours with my friend's big Jeep. I had put signs in the windows, big signs that said NEED A JACK and offered money. Nothing. Right as I was about to give up and start hitching, a Mexican family in a van pulled over, and the father bounded out.

He sized up the situation and called for his daughter, who spoke English. He conveyed through her that he had a jack but that it was too small for the Jeep, so we would need to brace it. Then he got a saw from the van and cut a section out of a big log on the side of the road. We rolled it over and put his jack on top, and we were in business.

I started taking the wheel off. Then, if you can believe it, I broke his tire iron—snapped the head clean off. No worries; he handed it to his wife, and she was gone in a flash down the road to buy a new tire iron. She was back in 15 minutes.

We finished the job, and I was a very happy man.

The two of us were filthy and sweaty. His wife produced a large water jug for us to wash our hands with. I tried to put a $20 bill in the man's hand, but he wouldn't take it, so instead, I went up to the van and gave it to his wife as quietly as I could. I asked the little girl where they lived. "Mexico," she said. They were in Oregon, so Mommy and Daddy could pick cherries for the next few weeks. Then they were going to pick peaches, then go home.

After I said my goodbyes and started walking back to the Jeep, the girl called out and asked if I had lunch. When I told her no, she ran up and handed me a tamale.

I thanked them again, walked back to my car, and opened the foil on the tamale. What did I find inside? My $20 bill! I ran to the van. The father saw the $20 in my hand and just started shaking his head no. With what looked like great concentration, he said in English, "Today you, tomorrow me."

By Justin Horner

4

Kindness
In Full Bloom

My parents met on St. Patrick's Day in 1944. Based on that, it's always been a special day of celebration for our family. The fact that Dad's grandparents met on the boat from Ireland to America only adds to the richness of our family history. We are Americans of Irish descent and proud of it. For us, the best part of Christmas Day is knowing that St. Patrick's Day is just around the corner.

It wasn't just about cardboard-cutout leprechauns and "Kiss Me I'm Irish" buttons, either. On this day of days, we feasted. Though ham and cabbage were a staple at our house, on Saint Patrick's Day, they shared tablespace with a fresh loaf of soda bread that Mom baked using my grandmother's recipe. And a steaming bowl of buttery colcannon potatoes crowned with a ring of brilliant green scallions. As a special treat, rice pudding laced with Irish cream whiskey rounded out the menu. Great and glorious St. Patrick himself would have found no warmer a welcome in America than the one he would have received at our home.

When I was first married and lived 3,000 miles from home, the memories of St. Patrick's Day warmed my heart as the icy wind of loneliness blew across the continent and chilled me to my soul. It was on our first St. Patrick's Day away from home that I sent my parents a dozen green carnations with a card that read, "Thanks for the memories." And so, a tradition began. I'm not sure when it happened, but somewhere along the way, Mom started sending me green carnations every year too.

Our company receptionist spent most of Valentine's Day paging one young lady after another to pick up various floral arrangements from adoring beaus, but I was the only one ever paged on St. Patrick's Day. I'd make my way to the lobby, cradle the bouquet in my arms, and stroll back to my office, imagining I was the envy of all, when in fact, nobody much noticed. But, oh, how special those green carnations made me feel, keeping the thrill of St. Patrick's Day alive in my heart. And time marched on.

The whirlwind of activity between October 2003 and February 2004 made my head spin. From the moment the doctor uttered the words "lung cancer," Mom and I spent all our time judging the decor of every medical office waiting room from one end of Philadelphia to the other. There was always one more test, one more scan, one more examination, and one more ray of hope until February 19th, when hope was lost, and Mom was gone.

Those were cold, dark days that followed her death and not just because it was the middle of the winter. I shuttled back and forth from work performing tasks by rote and barely connecting with family or friends. Mired in the grief of loss and loneliness, I hardly noticed the days getting longer or the warmth of the sun on my face.

As St. Patrick's Day inched closer, I turned a cold shoulder to it. My usual decorations stayed tucked away in their boxes. There would be no wearing of the green or baking of my grandmother's Irish soda bread. I'd let this St. Patrick's Day slide by without recognition. Take THAT, you dirty, rotten cancer!

When the day arrived, I scurried off to work, grabbed a cup of coffee, flipped on my computer, shut my office door, and hunkered down. In an hour, I heard a knock. When I looked up, Kathleen, the girl who occupied the office next door, peered at me through an inch-wide crack in the door.

"We have fresh scones out here and Irish soda bread. Can I get you something, Annie?"

"No, thanks," I said.

'Leave me alone,' I thought.

When lunchtime arrived, Kathleen tried again. "Annie, the cafeteria is having a St. Patrick's Day special. It's corned beef and cabbage. A bunch of us are going. Want to come?"

"No, thanks," I said.

"Don't you ever give up?" I thought.

And then in the quiet of the afternoon, I heard a page. "Annmarie Tait, please report to the lobby, you have a delivery."

Courier services frequently drop off paperwork to me, so I wasn't surprised, but I thought it a cruel twist of fate that today of all days, I'd been paged for a delivery.

The closer I got to the receptionist's desk, the more I thought my eyes were playing tricks on me. There on the counter, in a sheath of cellophane, rested a beautiful bouquet of Kelly-green carnations. It took my breath away, and my hands trembled as I opened the envelope and read the card pinned to the ribbon.

"May these lovely green carnations bloom forever in your heart." There was no signature.

I cradled the bouquet in my arms as I had so many times before and walked back to my office, wiping the tears from my eyes.

As I passed through each department, no one looked up, noticed, or said a word. I put the flowers in a vase and admired them, amazed by the whole experience. No bouquet ever meant more to me. It renewed my Irish spirit and helped me find the courage to carry on.

Somewhere in the darkness of my misery, a kind heart felt my pain and found a way to ease it with no desire for thanks or recognition. Despite my thorough interrogation, to this day, I don't know who sent them, but even St. Patrick would have to agree, this was a kindness of the highest order.

By Annmarie B. Tait

5

Blue Baby Blanket

Iwas at a meeting in a friend's house when the discussion turned to children. I was suddenly overcome with a mixture of past delight and present longing. My children were both grown, and my son, my youngest, was making plans to go off to college. My heart ached as I remembered him as a baby, how he liked to be pulled around in his wagon and how it felt to hold his hand as we went to the bus stop to meet my daughter after school. I could still hear his laughter as he splashed in the water at the beach. I thought of the many books we read at bedtime, both of us enjoying the words and the warmth of each other's company. When I looked down at my fingers, I half expected to see my nails tinted with red finger paint. I lost all track of the discussion as I was swept into this nostalgic reverie.

Then my friend brought me back abruptly as she thrust her toddler into my arms.

"Can you hold him for a minute?" she asked, not really waiting for an answer as she rushed to respond to the doorbell.

At first, my friend's son squirmed, looking around for his mother. But when he found a comfortable place to settle, he sat on my lap quite contentedly, his back resting against my chest. I felt waves of heat pulse through my sweater, a familiar sensation I used to love when my own children fell asleep in my arms. Once again, I pined for a past long gone.

As if responding to a signal, my friend's toddler turned his head so that he was looking directly at me. I looked back, amused, and said something in that voice adults use to entice children to smile. He didn't smile, just continued his gaze. His clear eyes compelled mine, and as we looked intently at each other, I knew something inside me shifted, that I had softened somehow. We stayed like that for a longer time than I thought a two-year-old could sustain. Then he wiggled out of my arms and went off across the room to where his sister was playing.

I thought he was going to join his sister's game, but he came back almost immediately, walking with that stumbling toddler urgency, his left arm outstretched. In his hand was his blue baby blanket. He held it solemnly out to me. I reached out and took it from him.

"Thank you," I said, this time in my most respectful adult voice, overwhelmed by his generosity and pre-verbal understanding. Without a word, he turned back to play while I held onto the blanket and rejoined the discussion.

When it was time to leave, I walked up to him and handed back the blanket. He smiled then, and I realized that kindness is inherent in us, at any age, if we allow ourselves to express it. The sadness was gone, replaced by an incredible feeling of connection and enhanced by the sweet comfort of a blue baby blanket.

By Ferida Wolff

6

The Man at
The Post Office

Random acts of kindness inspire me, and I love hearing stories about strangers doing good things for others. It makes my heart happy. I believe kindness is contagious and can spread like wildfire. In a world filled with darkness, random acts of kindness help me see the light and restore my faith in humanity. To me, kindness is a beautiful reminder that people still love and care for one another, despite everything else going on in the world. But I did not always feel this way. I changed the day a stranger decided to share his kindness with me.

The summer of 2011 was a long and stressful summer for my family. My husband was deployed to Afghanistan. I was working full time, and we had a seven-month-old son. I was also pregnant with our second child. I was an emotional wreck due to the pregnancy hormones and deployment. However, strength and hope kept me going, although sometimes strength and hope were hard to find. I felt heartbroken knowing that my husband was overseas, and my family was not complete for the time being. I could not fill the void he left behind. Tears rolled down my cheeks every time my son went through an infant milestone, and my husband was not physically there to watch it happen. More than ever, I needed physical and emotional support during the first months of my second pregnancy. "Why is this happening to our family? It's unfair we are not together," I asked myself. "People don't appreciate the sacrifices military families make for their freedom."

I tried to stay positive. I really did. But achieving a positive attitude was hard at times, especially when I felt lonely. My husband said his military brothers (men and women from his squadron at home) would offer to help and support me during the time he was gone, but no one, other than my own family, offered to help. I received no phone calls and no visits from his military family. Not even one encouragement card. Nothing. I was even unfriended from social media by some of his military "brothers" during his deployment. My loneliness turned into anger. I felt so angry at people. I was infuriated about their lack of support and their ungratefulness for my family's sacrifice for their freedom. My son was going growing out of infancy, and I was going through my second pregnancy alone because my husband was fighting a war overseas. People just didn't get how much my family was sacrificing.

On one hot summer Tucson afternoon, I put together a self-care package for my husband. I enclosed a greeting card that read "I miss you" and placed it on top of all the toiletries, baby wipes, and beef jerky that he requested I send to him. I strapped my son in his car seat, put the package in the car, and drove to the nearest post office. When we got there, the line was long, and my pregnant body was exhausted from working all day. The heat outside made me feel a lot worse. I felt like bursting into tears as I stood in that long line at the post office. I pushed my seven-month old's stroller with one hand and held the care package with the other, my sweaty arm wrapped around it. When the cashier finally called me up, I plopped the big box on the counter and said, "This package is going to Afghanistan." I then handed the cashier my money to pay for shipping. Suddenly, a man who appeared to be in his late 60s stepped out of the line and walked toward me, losing his place in line. He stood beside me at the counter. The cashier and I looked at each other and then at him, wondering what he wanted. I will never forget his face. He had visible wrinkles due to age and wore a red baseball cap and glasses. Then the man kindly told the cashier, "I want to pay for the package going to Afghanistan."

My eyes filled with tears, and my body became weak. I could not believe the kind act from this total stranger. A stranger who did not even know my name or my husband's name. He chose to lose his place in line to help me, an exhausted pregnant woman pushing a baby in a stroller, by paying for my husband's military package going overseas. I turned to look at the man (trying very hard not to cry) and said, "Thank you so much, sir. You don't know how much this means to me. Thank you." He then stepped back and returned to the line. I walked out of the post office and got in my car. I started to cry. I was utterly touched by this stranger's act of kindness. My husband's military "brothers" were not there for me, but this kind stranger was. "Some people do have big hearts," I told my son as we drove away. My own heart needed that reminder.

That summer, I learned that I could not count on people whom I know for help and support. However, my heart is happy when I think about strangers, like the man at the post office, jumping out of a long line to help another stranger who appears to be struggling in a time of need. I don't know this man's name, where he lives, what he does for a living, or if he is even alive today. All I know is that I often think about this kind stranger who touched my heart and inspired me to be kind to others. Every time I think about him, I send him love and light wherever he might be. This experience inspired me, and whenever the occasion presents itself, I carry out random acts of kindness. I usually perform the most random acts of kindness during the holiday season when people look for and believe in small miracles. I hope my acts of kindness will be a source of inspiration and move others as the man at the post office moved me.

Kindness is unquestionably contagious and leaves an imprint in the mind and heart. I will never forget the man at the post office.

By Bernadette Fleming

Chapter Two

DIVINE COMPASSION

There's always something to be grateful for.
Gratitude changes Everything.

—Anonymous

7

My Family's
Refugee Story

I was the fourth child born into an African family. My mother gave birth to eleven children—nine consecutive boys followed by two tomboy girls—in the village of Afikpo, in the southeastern region of Nigeria. My father, Isu okogeri, was a British-trained medical doctor and the traditional ruler of Afikpo. Dad and I were very close. My upbringing was greatly influenced by my father, with whom I had a profound affinity and from whom I learned much.

My mother, Chiyere Okogeri, was simply "Mom" in the real sense of the word. Her name, "Chiyere," means "God's gift." Her hands full with a rowdy brood of children, she was indeed God's gift to our family. My father was the leader and visionary for the family. Mom held the foundation together and provided the love, compassion, and understanding necessary to move the family forward.

Afikpo is a part of the Ibo (Igbo) ethnic group, one of the three major ethnic groups of Nigeria. The other two are the Hausa-Fulani in the North and the Yoruba in the southwest. Within these ethnic majorities, there are more than three hundred ethnic minority groups. The people of Afikpo engage predominantly in fishing and farming, producing primarily yams, rice, peanuts, cassavas, melons, corn, bananas, plantains, beans, palm oil, and palm wine. Afikpo cultural heritage is rich with colorful dances and festivals, including the famous Nkwa Umuagbogho (young female dancers), Nwa Nwite (female vocalists), and the Njenje and Iko festivals (harvest masquerade festivals).

The rich culture and relaxed atmosphere of Afikpo village provided a perfect setting for a peaceful existence. My family life was comfortable—even playful with so many siblings—for the first seven years of my life. That idyllic existence was changed forever when war set my homeland aflame.

Oil-rich Nigeria had a great future following its independence from the British in 1960. But, like countries colonized by Britain, as soon as the colonizer left, there was often a power struggle and civil war. In 1966, amid the escalating power struggle that engulfed Nigeria after independence, the country experienced its first military coup. During the coup, the first prime minister of an independent Nigeria, a northerner, as well as the first premier of the northern Nigeria region, were shot and killed, among other prominent northern military officers.

The anger fueled by the assassination of these prominent northern leaders evoked such uncontrollable rioting in northern Nigeria that more than 10,000 people were massacred. Since Igbo army officers had carried out the coup, Northerners turned on innocent Igbos (Easterners) who were residing in the North, launching indiscriminate reprisal attacks on Easterners. Hundreds of armed thugs broke into the area where Easterners lived and started burning, raping, looting, and killing men, women, and children from the East. With Igbos defending themselves, it turned into a bloodbath. There was a complete breakdown of law and order which the military was unable to restore.

Fearing for their lives, thousands of Igbos fled back to the southeast, their native home. When peaceful resolution to the growing political tension failed, and in the face of vengeful counter-coups by Northern soldiers in which many prominent Igbos were killed, and the Eastern region was rapidly being isolated by the Nigerian government, the Igbo leadership declared the Southeastern Nigerian province an independent sovereign nation henceforth known as Biafra. The announcement that Southeastern Nigeria, home of the Igbos, has seceded from the rest of the country provoked the Biafra-Nigeria civil war.

I was busy one day playing with my friends in my family compound at the age of seven, while my father sat a few feet away, conversing with his visitor, the newly appointed district officer of my village when suddenly earthshaking explosions were going off everywhere. I ran towards my parents in a panic, my heart pumping rapidly as the ferocious roar of low-flying fighter jets teared through the heavens in explosive crescendos. The very air shook and vibrated as the tremendous noise overshadowed every other sound. The ground was shaking with the intensity of a high magnitude earthquake as I ran into my mother's arms, who, together with my father, was calling on all the children to hurry and hide in nearby bushes. I was terrified, and perhaps for the first time in my life, solidly present in the moment, as I wondered if survival was possible. As the air raid continued, I looked up in the sky, while my mother held me, and saw huge trees snap like toothpicks, as bullets rained from the sky in every direction. My body quivered, and my heart was beating so fast and hard that I feared it would jump from my chest and drop on the ground. I had never been so terrified.

At one point, my father and his friend, the district officer of my village, couldn't tolerate the destruction any longer. They rose from where we were hiding to reenter our house, which was on the verge of collapsing, to retrieve dad's double-barreled shotguns. My mother was calling them back, reminding them of the imminent danger, but they wouldn't listen. Before long, in between the fighter jet's earthshaking explosions, we could hear the booms of double-barreled shotguns being fired. It was my father and his friend fighting back, somehow trying to take down fighter jets with shotguns! As they fired the shotguns, the district officer, speaking in my language, would nervously remind dad in a loud voice, "Doctor, we'd better shoot them down, or we'll soon be carrying our testicles in our own hands." The two men continued their retaliatory campaign until the air raid subsided. Remarkable, they didn't get hurt.

When the bombing was at its height, I didn't think we were going to die. I thought death was imminent. The question was, when? For a moment following the aerial bombing, there was silence in the village as the villagers waited patiently to see whether the fighter jets would return for more destruction or whether they were gone for good. Then suddenly, the town erupted into cries as people discovered that their family members and relatives were missing, wounded, or killed during the air assault. The terror in the air made the tragedy even more terrifying. My family was about to become refugees within a few hours, in a war that will claim more than 2 million civilian lives by starvation, and millions of more lives by bullets and explosives.

My village became extremely noisy and chaotic as I had never experienced or imagined, as people ran everywhere, in every direction, trying to figure out what was happening, how to escape and where to go. As some were busy wrapping the wounds of the wounded during the air raid, others stood helplessly wondering what to do with the dead, with so little time left to escape from the village. This was a scene that I never thought was possible, not only in my town but in my wildest imagination. Although the catastrophe broke my heart, I was unable to weep. Sometimes you get so hurt and scared that you can't cry even if you want to, because you are in a state of shock. Decisions had to be made at lightning speed and executed just as fast. You do what you can, and leave the rest in the hands of God, for the horror and atrocities of being a civilian in the Biafra-Nigeria war zone was unimaginable. The enemy was cruel. Enemy war planes relentlessly bombed civilians, civilian centers, and even refugee camps throughout the Igboland.

As villagers scrambled to escape, you could hear some of the elderly asking in my language, "Ayi mere gini?" (What have we done?), as they trekked with their few belongings out of the village. They were confused and horrified.

Later that day, my family and most Afikpo people evacuated the village and became refugees in nearby cities. I remember my parents hurrying everyone to pack just a few things because our cars, a Peugeot and a British Humber Super Snipe, could only take so much. As dad was busy packing, trying to sort out the most important things to take along, I was right at his side, as I always was in those days. Although I was a child, I sometimes acted and behaved like my father's guardian, like his other half.

"Remember to bring some money," I said solemnly. I suppose it was my way of assuring my family's protection and support. Just as solemnly, he responded, "Yes, son, I will."

As we began our journey out of the village, there were patches of dark smoke everywhere from burning houses and trees. The air was filled with a repulsive odor that came from a mixture of burning bamboo and palm trees, explosives, and everything else that was aflame. Burning sounds rebounded from raffia rooftops, burning bushes, and dust from collapsed houses hovered in the air. The streets were packed with fleeing refugees, carrying few belongings on their heads in massive columns that stretched for miles. While some carried their agricultural produce, others carried live chickens and goats. Women tied their children on their backs with terry cloth.

Just when the streets were congested by fleeing refugees, the fighter jets returned to bomb the civilians. As a result, many villagers never made it out of Afikpo alive. In the history of my village, this was by far the greatest disaster its people had ever experienced. I couldn't think. My mind was busy recording the images, which are still very alive in my mind today.

My family escaped safely from Afikpo, and for the next three years, we were on the run as refugees. Although we moved to a new village or city in the eastern region, now a part of Biafra, every three to six months, to avoid capture or destruction by the enemy, I was grateful that no family member was hurt.

By Zeal Okogeri

8

The War Intensified

By the time my family moved to a city called Okwele, the Nigeria-Biafra civil war was at its height. There was no long-distance communication system during the war. Usually, if you met someone in the marketplace, you began asking questions. "Where had they come from?" "Whom had they seen?" Also, when a new set of refugees moved into the area, we asked whether they had seen a specific person or family. That was how news spread: by word of mouth and by the coincidence of running into the right people.

In this way, we learned that my paternal grandmother, Nnesundae, had died. Her death was caused in part by the stresses of the war. It was a sad time for all of us. Happier news was that my maternal grandmother was alive. Arrangements were later made for my mother and grandmother to connect. Our grandmother was also relieved to find out that we were alive and well, for she too had been worried.

One day my mother, my oldest brother, and a village neighbor who had escaped Afikpo with my family went on foot to a local market. We had long ago abandoned our cars due to a lack of spare parts for needed repairs. It was a distant market, about four hours by foot round-trip along dusty, unpaved roads, but it was the only marketplace where a variety of foods was available.

We might have had to walk on foot to a distant market, but we were luckier than most in that we did not starve. There was such a scarcity of food during the war that more than two million civilians died from starvation. At a refugee camp near where we lived, I saw children and adults whose heads were resting on bare bones. They had not eaten a real meal in months. From a distance, you could count their ribs, and, in fact, their entire vertebrae. There was hardly any flesh left on their bodies. Many were infected with diseases in addition to a myriad of other health problems, yet they remained alive. I realized then that human beings have an incredible ability to survive. There were relief efforts by the Red Cross and other humanitarian agencies from around the world, which were greatly appreciated. But often during the distribution of food, many refugees, having starved for a long time, would fight over the food. Unfortunately, those who desperately needed to be fed were too weak to fight for their food. The tragedy of war is that those who had nothing to do with the decisions that led to war suffer the most.

That day, while my mother, brother, and our neighbor went in search of food, one of the most devastating military aerial bombings of the war took place. In Okwele village, the fighter planes were so relentless that those of us who remained took cover under trees and bushes for practically the entire day. The shelling and automatic weapons fire went on for hours. We could hear heavy machine-gun fire from the military barracks located a few miles from our refugee home. That day marked the climax of the war for us. It seemed the enemy was determined to level and obliterate everything. At the end of the air raid, many lives were lost, as usual, and much property destroyed. By then, we had seen so many brutal and senseless killings of innocent civilians that we'd become desensitized.

However, following the bombing at Okwele, we worried about my mother, brother, and neighbor at the open marketplace. We waited all day for them to return, but they were nowhere in sight. The night was growing dark. Since there was no electricity, there was complete darkness by 7 p.m. That night, we got news from people who returned from a village located close to the market area. They reported that the air raid had killed every single person at that market.

That was the first time I ever saw my father shaken. He shouted, "That's impossible!"

My brothers and I panicked and collapsed to the floor, crying. As practiced in my culture, my father took a bottle of palm wine to the side of the house and started calling on every ancestral spirit he knew. He called on some names and oracles I had never heard him call upon before. He poured the wine continuously on the ground, engaging in libation and asking the spirits how such a tragedy could be possible. After about an hour of incantations, he came back to the house and reported that our late grandfather had appeared and reassured him that no family member had been hurt in the air raid. Of course, we dismissed his report. We thought he was only trying to calm everybody, as well as to maintain his own emotional balance. In the meantime, I, at eight years old, prayed myself to exhaustion, asking God to bring my mother home.

About 9:00 that evening, I heard my mother's voice. Out of the darkness walked she, my brother, and our neighbor.

They were returning from the market with baskets on their heads. You cannot imagine our joy. From that moment on, a deep part of me was devoted to this sacred essence that we call God, for It had delivered my most precious wish. I couldn't have imagined what life would be like without my mother.

By Zeal Okogeri

9

The War Ends

In January 1970, after all the bloodshed, millions of lost lives, disease infestations, massive destruction, and homelessness, the Nigeria-Biafra civil war was over. Biafra surrendered. It was time to return home to Afikpo, my village, from our refugee home in Umudi. My family members and hundreds of other refugees boarded and were transported in enclosed, windowless forty-foot trailers, the type of trailers used by retail stores to convey cargo. Our destination was Okigwe, a city about fifty miles from my village. There were no seats in the trailer, only standing room. We were packed like sardines in a can, and breathing was difficult during the three-hour journey. We felt every bump as the trailer galloped on the dirt road, and whenever the driver made a sudden stop to avoid a pothole, everyone in the container would fall over one another. When the driver took off again, we would all fall in the opposite direction.

On the one hand, I was happy the war was over and that we were going home. But on the other hand, I wasn't sure my brothers and I would survive the ride home. The container was dark and hot, with little circulating air. Some of the refugees suffocated in the cargo trailer. Miraculously, my brothers and

I survived the horrific ride to our destination, a refugee camp in Okigwe.

We stayed at the refugee camp for about a month before the new government arranged transportation for us to return to Afikpo. Okigwe refugee camp was an open campground. Each family had a small, designated space where its members slept on bare ground. No mattresses or even sheets were available to spread over the dusty earth. Many returning refugees died at the camp in Okigwe. The first thing you saw every morning upon arising from sleep was dead refugees as they were being carried away for burial by volunteers. Due to poor hygiene of the refugee environment, we almost lost one of my older brothers. He was infected with tapeworm. Fortunately, he made a remarkable recovery.

When we arrived in our hometown, Afikpo, we discovered the village had become a ghost town. Because of the massive destruction, it wasn't easy to recognize the once-familiar surroundings. Once Afikpo had been a mixture of modernization alongside antiquity—houses constructed with mud and topped with raffia roofs, as well as similarly constructed public "pit" toilets, sat just blocks from modern homes with amenities such as television, comfortable furniture, and modern toilet facilities. Now there was ubiquitous devastation.

When we reached the location of our house, trees were growing in what used to be our living room. We had to navigate through weeds six feet high to find the bedrooms. Our property—piano, organ, furniture, and everything left behind—was destroyed. There were debris and paper everywhere, mostly hardened and stuck to the floor due to the many showers of rain and sunshine of the past three years.

As we all stood there gazing at the destruction, my mother couldn't take it anymore. She broke down and started crying. I remembered my father calling upon her, "What are you crying for?" "Don't cry. Be thankful that God brought us home alive. Don't worry; we'll rebuild." Like everyone else in the village, we had to start over.

Once again, my father commenced operating his clinic and church. My brothers and I worked hard, helping Papa treat patients in exchange for agricultural produce because no one had money after the war. We had some leftover Biafran currency, but they were now illegal tenders. The government required all Biafran currencies burnt. Until there was access to Nigerian currency, we had to use the barter system. Some of us would help by collecting clean water for botanical and homeopathic tinctures, some would assist dad in their preparation, and others would hand the finished remedies to patients. It was like an assembly line.

There was no roof on our house immediately following the war. We used palm tree branches for shelter by placing them across the few walls that were still standing. Whenever it rained during the night, family members would wake up to find themselves sleeping in a pond of water. We would spend the rest of the night until morning scooping away water and trying to find a dry spot. Although we endured physical and psychological trauma to a scale few can imagine, there was no reason to complain. We were happy the war was finally over and faithful we would one day recover from our losses.

We continued working hard, and gradually we rebuilt. New houses, a clinic, and a church were later built in our compound. As our economy improved, some of my siblings were sent to the United States, Greece, and India to study medicine, law, business, and science, respectively.

I learned a lot from the war, especially about 'gratitude' and 'resilience.' By recognizing and appreciating the relentless generosities of Spirit—divine compassion, we galvanized the hope and faith to keep going. In other words, I learned that after you get knocked down, you need to get up, brush yourself off, and get back to what you were doing before.

After my family endured such unimaginable hardship during the war, lost everything, returned home, rebuilt, and within five years, my siblings were traveling abroad, one after the other to study in universities, paid for by my family, I knew then that anything is possible. I realized then that human beings could transcend seemingly insurmountable obstacles and triumph under the most debilitating conditions.

By Zeal Okogeri

10

Elementary School Student Bails His Teacher Out of Jail

My family made a rapid economic recovery after the Nigeria-Biafra civil war, which attracted the attention of the new military government, thanks to our neighbors. The period following the civil war was a tense time. Soldiers patrolled the streets, and anyone could be arrested for practically any reason and detained based solely on secret evidence. Any well-established civilian was also considered a potential threat to the new government. About eight months following our return to Afikpo, two military Land Rovers arrived at our family compound with six soldiers armed with machine guns. The soldiers arrested my father on the spot. They instructed him to board one of the Land Rovers. Upon asking where the soldiers were taking him, they simply instructed him to enter the jeep.

At this point, Dad felt his life was potentially in danger. He asked to have at least one family member accompany him. That way, if anything were to go wrong, there would be someone to give an account to the village. After much deliberation, the soldiers agreed on one family escort. You can probably guess who my father chose as his companion. I jumped nervously into the backseat of the Land Rover with my father. Upset by the development, my mother and the rest of the family members ran after the jeeps as they sped away to an undisclosed location. It was an eerie journey. No one talked. The soldiers had obviously been instructed not to communicate with us. Dad's expression showed he was concerned about the family he had left behind.

We boarded the jeep at my family compound around 6 p.m. By the time we reached our destination, it was almost midnight. I was quite distressed by the whole affair. By this time, I was nine years old. I couldn't understand why we were being subjected to more suffering after enduring the atrocities of the war. I asked my father what had happened and was disappointed by his explanation.

"Our neighbors reported to the army that I was making unusual financial progress while everyone else was still struggling," he explained calmly. He said I should sleep and not worry too much about it. How could I sleep when I knew my father was in trouble?

About 7:00 the next morning, the police transferred us to the central prison in Enugu city, where we started to serve our jail sentence for an undisclosed offense. On our way to the new prison, I looked out the window and noticed many cars on the road with civil servants rushing to work. Street vendors were busy selling newspapers, fried food, and soft drinks, which were all refreshing to me because my village, Afikpo, was not as developed as Enugu. I was starving. We had not eaten for almost a whole day. From the jeep, I could smell the savory fried foods, like plantains (fried bananas). Momentarily, my mind wandered to Mom's delicious cooking, but it was not for long. We had arrived at the new prison, which was filled with Biafran war prisoners and others, most of them completely naked and filthy. Sanitation was so poor; the entire police station smelled like a filled toilet that was left unflushed for a month. It was apparent the cells were not equipped with functional toilet facilities. The appearance of the prisoners was nauseating. Monkeys caged in the zoo were in paradise compared to the prisoners.

Fortunately, my father and I were detained in a separate area, away from the filth. In contrast to the detention area of other prisoners, you could say that we received VIP treatment. The police were aware of my dad's social status. They demonstrated respect by detaining him away from the filth. Still, despite the cleaner detention area, we could not escape the odor, nor the obscenities that were part of the prisoners' vocabulary. It was overwhelming. Many of the prisoners were crying and begging my dad to help them.

Since there was no charge against me, the police allowed me to wander out of prison and walk about the police barracks. By some good fortune, the chief of police was compassionate toward me; he called me over and gave me some money to buy food from the street vendors. I went out to the street and purchased some fried peanuts, and Fanta orange soft drinks from the street vendors then brought them back for Dad. The money was not enough to buy the fried plantains I had hoped to enjoy, but I made do. When I returned, my father looked worried. I could tell he was concerned because when he worried, he didn't say much. I felt sad and wished he would somehow be rescued. Luck was on our side. The news of Dad's detention had spread around Enugu like wildfire. It was the talk of the town, we later learned.

Dad was well known among civil servants in the eastern region because, before going to England to study medicine in the early 1960s, he had been a schoolteacher, and later became Inspector of Schools for the eastern region of Nigeria.

This position brought him in contact with all schools in the eastern region.

The news of our detention reached one of my father's former elementary school students, who was now a well-established civil servant living in Enugu with his wife and two children. He couldn't believe his ears when someone informed him that the police were detaining Dr. Okogeri. He rushed to the police station to verify that this man was the same Okogeri, who had taught him in Elementary Six. When he met my father in prison, it was such a moving moment. He screamed out of sheer excitement at the sight of Dad, then rushed to hug his elementary school teacher to whom he credited his professional success. Dad, on the other hand, could hardly recognize his former pupil, now himself a father.

The man quickly negotiated with the police, paid my father's fine, and bailed us out of prison. He then invited us to meet his wife and children. His wife was pleasant. She prepared a feast of steamed rice with a spicy fresh fish stew in coconut sauce and a separate dish of pounded yam with egusi soup—fine Nigerian dishes. For a nine-year-old boy who had not seen a proper meal in days, I was quite delighted. The meal was so satisfying that I fell asleep shortly after. We spent two days with this family. In the meantime, Dad's former pupil arranged for our transportation to Afikpo and gave us presents to take home to our family.

It was a great pleasure to rejoin my family in the village. To be able to play with my siblings and friends once again was a source of tremendous exhilaration. My gratitude to my father's elementary school student and the Divine was boundless.

Sometimes people are in a hurry to reap the fruits of their labor, or the seeds of their kindness, not realizing that nature takes care of all that. Dad reaped the rewards of his services as a schoolteacher 25 years later!

By Zeal Okogeri

11

My First Plane Ride

When I was a teenager, living in Afikpo village in southeastern Nigeria, my father traveled abroad every year to attend medical conferences. Upon his return, he would share with the family incredible stories of his experiences in Europe, Asia, North America, and South America. Fascinated by his stories, I pestered him for years: "I want to go to Alibeke with you." Alibeke, in Afikpo language, literally translates to "the land of white people."

One day he sent for me to come to see him at the clinic. I thought he needed help, someone to deliver medicine to his patients. But the news I was about to receive would change my life forever. When I entered his office, he sat me down and said he arranged for a photographer to take my passport photographs.

"For what purpose?" I asked.

"For your new international passport," he said. "You are traveling with me to Belgium, England, the Netherlands, and the United States. We'll attend medical conferences in the United Kingdom and the Netherlands, and then we'll proceed to the United States to visit your older brother."

He had more details, but I was too excited to listen any

further. I ran out of his office, jumping up and down, yelling, "Yeah! Yeah! Yeah!"

I was so happy that, within a few minutes, everybody I saw, even strangers, knew I was going to Alibeke. For one to be able to travel abroad is a great privilege in my village. It's an even greater privilege for a teenager to receive the opportunity of overseas travel. I couldn't believe I was going to experience Alibeke.

As the first term was about to end, all my friends in secondary school knew of my planned voyage. I was to return before school resumed the following term. My friends were as excited as I was. I promised to bring back lots of photos and souvenirs from Europe and America.

As the date of departure grew closer, it became impossible for me to sleep at night due to my uncontrollable excitement and anticipation. I had never been abroad before, and my imagination was running wild. Everything I knew about the outside world was based on my geography class in elementary school, and the stories brought back by my father after his voyages.

Finally, the day arrived for our departure. We were driven from Afikpo, to Enugu airport, about 50 miles from my town. From there, we boarded a Nigeria Airways flight to Lagos, the former capital of Nigeria. The new capital is Abuja.

At age 14, this was my first time seeing an airplane on the ground and my first time to fly in a plane – and if I had had a choice, it would have been my last. As soon as our twin-engine propeller-type aircraft took off from Enugu airport, heavy rain started. We were traveling during the rainy season. The rainy season in Nigeria can be severe. Fifteen minutes into our flight, the plane started galloping like a truck on an unpaved road full of potholes. Soon, it felt as though the plane was flying sideways. There were lightning and heavy thunderstorms. The turbulence was so rough that many passengers were giving up hope. While some raised their hands in prayer, others were crying and shouting, "We are not going to make it!"

The Muslim passengers were calling upon Allah, while the Christians were screaming for Jesus. It was pure chaos in expression. As this was my very first flight, I didn't know what to make of the commotion. I turned and looked at my father to determine if this was a typical scene in an aircraft. But he, too, was busy praying. At this point, I realized this was not an everyday plane ride. I was getting worried and asked him to pull down the window shade. The lightning was making me nervous. Since the praying passengers had transformed the cabin into an interfaith church, I felt I could probably use some praying myself.

To make the situation even more unpleasant, the pilot announced over the intercom that he just received instructions to divert the flight to a nearby airport in Ibadan, which is close to Lagos, and "try" to land there. With that announcement, an uproar erupted in the plane. In a chorus, the passengers sighed, "Heeyii!" (This is one of the Nigerians' expressions of despair.)

"You see, I told you we're not going to make it," a pessimistic passenger sitting in front of us reminded his wife. The pilot continued his struggle through the storm. At times, it felt as if we were floating above our seats as the plane made sudden drops in altitude. Finally, with wings wagging, the pilot slammed the aircraft onto the runway of the Ibadan airport. Passengers were cheering and clapping for the pilot and proclaiming, "God is wonderful!"

When I stepped out of the plane, it wasn't easy to walk. I felt like I had just completed a long roller coaster ride at an amusement park. Upon entering the airport lobby, Dad took me to a newsstand and bought me my first inspirational book, *The Power of Right Thought* by Ella Wheeler Wilcox.

I gladly accepted it. "Who knows how many more of these crazy rides there will be in the future?" I wondered.

The weather cleared up two hours later. Nervously we boarded the same aircraft. The plane was almost empty this time because most of the passengers elected to complete their journey by road. However, we landed safely in Lagos without encountering much turbulence.

Phew!

This was my initiation into air travel.

By Zeal Okogeri

Chapter Three

LOVE
IN ACTION

When we practice loving kindness and compassion,
we are the first ones to profit.

— Rumi

12

For Love
and Love Alone

So, there we were, in 1976: four young people stranded on the border of Nebraska and Colorado, victims of a snapped timing chain in our car. The car shop said it would be two weeks before the car would be ready, and we still had 170 miles to travel to get to my brother's cabin, located in the foothills of the mountains just west of Denver.

Hitching a ride became our only option. After an hour with no success, we decided to split up into groups of two. Our two other friends quickly found a ride, but my girlfriend and I were still unsuccessful, and our spirits were sinking fast as we baked on the side of the road under the blazing Colorado summer sun.

Suddenly, it looked like a car was pulling over toward us, finally! We started grabbing our stuff until I noticed that the car that was pulling over was a Volkswagen beetle with two people in front and the back seat filled to the brim with stuff! My heart fell as I started wondering why this guy had even pulled over in the first place.

The driver jumped out with a big smile on his face and cheerfully asked, "So, need a lift?"

"Uh, yeah," I said. "Our car broke down, and we need to get to Denver—but...uh, where you going to put us?"

"Oh, in the back seat," he said. "Just give me a few minutes to rearrange things a bit."

What followed next is something I'll never forget. He suddenly became a flurry of arms, pulling stuff out of the back seat, throwing it onto the side of the road, then opening the hood of the VW (which was the actual trunk of the car, since the engine was in the back) and emptying that as well, in the same almost maniacal, but still happy manner. Then, he started putting it all back, scrunching things here and there, like piecing together a puzzle until, almost a full half-hour later, he had managed to clear a small space in the back seat where we were, I think, supposed to fit!

"There," he said proudly. "I think you'll be able to get in there."

Well, I'm 6 foot 3 inches tall, and my girlfriend was tall, too, and I must say, I had second thoughts as we started the process of wedging ourselves into the back seat, finally fitting, although my knees ended up almost touching my chest! I figured, though, you know, "Any port in a storm." And off toward Denver we went!

Our driver was undoubtedly a jolly fellow, whistling, and pleasantly chatting with us as we drove along. However, with no air conditioning in the car (remember, this was a VW bug, 1976), it seemed like the temperature in the back was around 100. My girlfriend and I were sweating profusely, and my knees were screaming for a different position!

Mercifully, I saw that we were finally getting close to

Denver. The driver then asked, "So where exactly does your brother live?"

"Oh," I said, "actually, about 20 miles up into the mountains from Denver, but just drop us off at the next gas station, and we'll give him a call." Now, remember, this was 1976, before pagers or cell phones, so waiting at a payphone was probably going to be our fate if my brother wasn't home when we called.

He said, "So, do you know how to get to his cabin?" "Well, yeah," I replied, "but sir, you've already gone out of your way just to make us fit into your car! I'm sure you'd like to get on your way, and besides, we're talking about 20 more miles of gravely mountain roads. To be honest, I don't know if your little bug here, stuffed to the gills like it is and with all of us, could even make it up those steep roads!

"Well," he said, looking back at us with a cheerful smile, "let's find out—my friend here and I love a good adventure!" As further protests on my part kept falling on deaf ears, off we went, up into the mountains, all the time wondering if indeed there was a way this adventure could have a happy ending!

Sure enough, about an hour and many silent prayers later, there we were—the dusty little VW bug pulling into the driveway of my brother's cabin!

As our driver helped pull us (literally) out of the back seat, he happily said, "Yup, now that WAS an adventure, wasn't it?" I smiled weakly as the blood finally started to flow back into my numb knees. Then, as I moved to pull out my wallet to give him some compensation for going way above and beyond the call of duty, a firm hand clamped down on my wrist, forcing my wallet back into my pocket. He said, "No, there'll be none of that now!"

"But sir," I pleaded, "after dozens and dozens of huge cars with only one driver passed us by, you chose to give us a ride although there wasn't room in your car, and it took you almost a half hour just to make some space available. Then, you go way out of your way up into the mountains with a small car loaded to the gills on a blazing summer day, not even knowing if we would make it. There must be some way I can repay you!"

He thought for a moment, then looked me directly in the eyes. Smiling, he said, "Actually, there is something you could do that would make me very happy."

"Name it," I said.

"If you find yourself in a situation," he said, "where you could help someone in need like I just helped you, then please do it for love and love alone."

I trembled a little inside as he spoke, realizing this was something I would actually do and never forget.

"You got it," I said. With that, we all hugged, he got back in his little VW bug, and they drove off down the dusty mountain road, waving and smiling.

Since that one amazing hot summer's day in Colorado, I can't tell you how many times I have chosen to offer my help to others in need. When I do, I see his smiling face and hear those beautiful words, "For love and love alone."

By John Villemonte

13

Kindness,
A Personal Perspective

Kindness, an essential human characteristic, is something innately woven into the DNA of every human being.

Personally, this essential characteristic is a fulfilling and refreshing part of my existence. I have shown this attribute in many ways and to many people, even strangers whom I cannot begin to count. However, despite the spontaneity of this expression, one example readily comes to mind. I will, for this anthology, try to narrate the story.

In Nigerian, I was approached for help by a dynamic young man whom I knew as a hardworking, honest person. He had been struggling to maintain his family—a wife and three children – with earnings from the most ubiquitous but dangerous means of public transportation, called "Okada."

Okada is a motorbike, the most common means of transport for the massive population of struggling, everyday people who do not have private cars and who cannot afford the luxury of taxi cabs. This young man, whom I will call Jacob, owned the 'ladies' model of this motorbike, and this was not the preference of commuters. Most commuters preferred the more masculine, stronger, and seemingly more comfortable model, which could also carry more than one passenger at a time. Hence, those who owned the more masculine model got more passengers and made more money. Jacob came and explained this difference in earnings to me. He could not afford to buy the preferred model, and this was having a serious financial impact as he struggled to raise his family. The cost of the model he wanted was 80,000 Nigerian Naira, about 600 U.S. dollars at the time. He lamented and agonized over the refusal of his well-to-do family members to help him.

I am not a close family member, but he said that he felt certain unexplained confidence that I may be sympathetic to his needs. Jacob pleaded that if I could render assistance, his family's deplorable financial situation would greatly improve. He assured me that he would make monthly payments of 10,000 naira into my bank account in Nigeria until the loan was repaid.

I was skeptical but was moved with compassion, a characteristic quality, to help make a positive difference in the well-being of this struggling young man. Jacob's request for financial help also provided an opportunity for self-education of the perennial struggles of ordinary folks in the harsh Nigerian socioeconomic environment. It brought home the apparent lack of opportunities in the society. Indeed, there was an economic disadvantage for the owners of the ladies' model of the Okada—the only hope of public transportation in a country with a rapidly degrading and inefficiently maintained infrastructure.

I summoned courage, allowed the flow of the milk of

human kindness to wash through my body, and asked Jacob to visit the next day to pick up a check for 80,000 Naira. His feeling of relief, gratitude, and grace was as spontaneous as it was contagious. I quickly felt a spiritual nudge that I was about to make a positive impact on the life of another human being. This was as refreshing as it was fulfilling. A spiritual experience, indeed.

Jacob picked up his check, with no interest or any harsh conditions attached, and quickly purchased a brand-new Okada. Unknown to me, he spread the story of his newfound goodwill around town. That was not as important to me as the fact that Jacob worked hard with his new motorbike; he improved the financial health of his family and consistently repaid his loan, as promised, with impeccable gratitude, humility, and grace.

Jacob taught me, with his strength of character and honesty, that there are many good and honorable people in a society often associated with corruption.

Jacob continued his show of gratitude, even after fully repaying his loan. He visited me every Christmas to say thank you with bottles of red wine. I told him to stop, insisting that the yearly Christmas gifts were unnecessary.

His response was:

"I will not stop! You came to my rescue when everybody I approached for help rejected me, even those who had more money than you."

This was touching and again gave me the sense that my show of kindness made a difference in the lives of Jacob and his family.

Yes, let us not relent in showing kindness to our fellow human beings as much as we can. It is best and spiritually rewarding when it is freely given without direct reciprocal expectations.

I am gratified to have shown kindness to Jacob; it made me a better person, just as it made him and his family better people. Even with occasional ingratitude from those to whom we have shown kindness, it remains a spiritual virtue that will continue to make the world a better place.

By Charles Onunkwo

14

The Cambodian Kitten

It was the last day of my one-week journey to Cambodia. Having visited some of the most charming and beautiful places in the country, I had no plans other than enjoying my leisure time and sunshine, then leaving the country in the evening.

After a wonderful lunch, I enjoyed the afternoon wandering the streets and taking pictures. It was a quiet area and not far from the city center, so I decided to walk to the local market. While passing a beautiful home, I noticed a kitten sitting alone in front of the gate, meowing loudly. When I squatted to pet her, I realized she could not stand; one leg was injured, causing her pain. Also, she could barely keep her left eye open because it was infected and full of thick mucus discharge. I asked the girls in the yard if the kitten was theirs; they shook their heads. The poor little thing shouldn't be left on streets alone under such a high temperature and humidity, so I picked her up, cradled her in my arms, and asked a tuk-tuk driver to take me to the nearest animal hospital.

A kind female doctor checked the cat's eye and leg carefully. Fortunately, her leg was not broken. The doctor gave me some eye drops and pain medication. I asked if the doctor could take care of the kitten for a while until she found someone to adopt her. She shrugged and explained that she was unable to keep the kitten in the clinic. She suggested that I send the cat to a temple in the city; maybe some monks could take care of her. I was glad to hear that, so I bought some cat food to take along with me. The veterinarian wrote a note in Cambodian for me to show taxi drivers, in case their English wasn't so good. She also wrote instructions for me to give the monks, for administering the eye drops and pills.

I was on the streets again under the intense sunshine, holding the small kitten in my hands. She was so adorable, trembling, but staying strong through the whole ordeal. I stopped the first taxi I saw, showed the driver the note, and explained my situation. The look on his face turned from doubtful to delight, and he agreed. We arrived at the temple rather quickly. I walked behind the driver as he looked around the monastery for the monks. Unfortunately, most of the monks were out for study, and the two we met weren't interested.

We drove to another temple, and the same thing happened. I was frustrated and felt helpless; however, the driver wouldn't give up. He drove us to a third temple. When we entered this older temple, unlike the other monasteries, there were large trees in the yard that provided much-needed shade. It felt peaceful, and I liked the place immediately. I was further encouraged when the tuk-tuk driver revealed that he was a monk at this monastery when he was a young boy and has friends here. In their dormitory, we met three monks in different stages of life: an old man, a teenager, and a child. They had already raised some cats and a dog and said, without hesitation, that they would keep the kitten. The old monk began studying the note on how to administer the drugs while the teenage monk put a plate on the table and opened the bag of cat food that I brought. The child monk was fascinated with this new little friend and watched her gobble her food. I was excited that we found such a nice home for the kitten. Before leaving the temple, I exchanged WeChat information with the teenage monk so he could keep me updated with the kitten's progress.

The tuk-tuk driver had spent almost two hours with me as we drove around looking for a home for the kitten. When he later dropped me off at the market, he neither complained that I had wasted his time nor ask for more money, although this was a prime travel season when there was a great opportunity to earn lots of money. His kindness touched me deeply. The kitten must have grown on him, and, like me, he wanted it to have a happy home.

I'm from Tianjin, China, and this was my first visit to Cambodia. Throughout my stay in Cambodia, the people I met, especially the tuk-tuk drivers, were very kind to me. They made me feel at home. I learned from this journey that when you don't see yourself as just a tourist when you travel, you'll experience more than you expected.

Being kind to animals, like taking a cat or dog off the street, giving them a home and bonding with them, can be a most rewarding experience.

By Zhang Yue

15

Your Bird Will Be Fine

Having been a flight attendant for 45 years before retiring a few years ago, I have so many stories about my experiences. Some are entertaining, funny, and unbelievable, while others are very serious and unfortunate, such as a medical emergency in the air. We were flying to Atlanta International Airport when a male passenger had a severe epileptic seizure. We had to call paramedics ahead of time to meet our plane at the Atlanta airport, where the passenger was supposed to catch a connecting flight to his home in Zurich, Switzerland.

When the emergency medical team boarded the plane, did their physical exams, and began carrying the gentleman off to an ambulance that was parked next to the plane, the passenger kept asking me over and over, "What about my bird?" He was very upset, frustrated, and panicking. I had no idea what he was talking about, as much I tried to make sense of it. As it turned out, he had his beloved bird, a colorful little cockatoo, in a pet carrier tucked away under his seat. He was very worried about the welfare of the bird now that he was on his way to the hospital. When I was married, my husband had a parrot, so I was very familiar with taking care of a bird. I told him not to worry, that I would gladly take the bird home with me and care for it until he was well enough to go home. I reassured him that since I had a bird before, I knew all about taking care of one. This was a source of great relief for the passenger. We exchanged names and phone numbers so I could call him, not only to update him on his bird but also to check up on him. At that point, he was able to relax and allow the emergency medical team to carry him to the ambulance.

On my way home from the airport, I stopped at a pet store and bought some bird feed. When we got home, I dusted off a birdcage that I had in the garage. The bird seemed quite happy in his new cage, which I hung in my living room.

Four days later, I got an early call from the passenger, telling me that he was being discharged from the hospital shortly and would be taking a flight home to Zurich that evening. We made plans to meet at a designated location at the airport to reunite him with his beautiful cockatoo so they could fly home together. He was happy to see his bird, which was in great condition, and he couldn't thank me enough for my kindness and generosity. He knew that what I had done was beyond my call of duty as a flight attendant. Two weeks later, I received a lovely thank you letter from Switzerland. The gentleman said he was feeling fine and that he and his bird were happy to be back home after the drama in Atlanta.

By Beverly Mackay

16

Selfless Stranger on the Plane

The pilot's voice came over the loudspeaker, urging the passengers to take their seats. Aggravated travelers shuffled down the cramped aisle, shoving large carry-on bags into stuffed overhead compartments. A mechanical issue had caused a 40-minute delay, and people openly complained about tight connections. I pushed my backpack under the seat in front of me and fastened my seatbelt, the new book I'd brought for the trip resting on my lap. It was then that I saw her.

She wore a long silk tunic and matching pants with intricate gold stitching along her neckline and wrists. A beautiful headscarf draped over her dark hair, framing her delicate face. With an infant in one arm, she pulled a rolling bag behind her while urging the small child in front of her to move forward. Though her words were spoken in a language I did not know; the gentle tones were those of a mother.

The child moved slowly, occasionally stopping to pick up something interesting from the floor. The mother continued her soft coaxing despite the irritated sighs of the travelers behind her. Finally, they reached their seats just a few rows ahead of me, but the mother's challenge had just begun. Her toddler shrieked as she tried to buckle her seat belt. That woke the baby, who started to cry. The procession of passengers abruptly stopped, the mother and her carry-on bag blocking the aisle. Tension filled the cabin as exasperated sighs and muttered comments chilled the air. A flight attendant appeared, cramming the woman's bag into an overheard compartment and asking that she please take her seat. The baby wailed, and I shifted uncomfortably in my seat, remembering a similar experience of my own many years before.

Our twins were just a year old when my husband and I took them on a three-hour flight to Florida. Struggling at the airport with a double stroller, two car seats, and an overflowing diaper bag, I was exhausted before the flight began. When we finally boarded the plane, a babe in my husband's arms, and one in my own, I couldn't help but notice the familiar expression on the faces of our fellow travelers. Their eyes begged, "Please don't sit here," as we proceeded down the aisle. I knew the look. I had been guilty of it myself.

Once we were settled, my husband and I took turns passing toys and snacks between us. For the first hour, both babies were content on our laps, but as the second hour began, the daughter in my arms became fussy. All efforts to entertain her failed, and my anxiety escalated with her cries. My husband sat helplessly across the aisle; our other daughter asleep in his arms. There was no reprieve or tag-teaming lest we risk awaking the second baby. It was up to me to subside the volcano rupturing in my arms. Soon she was inconsolable.

I rocked her and bounced her, speaking quietly into her ear as she screamed and pulled against me. My seatmate shifted toward the window, raising his book higher as if to create a sound barrier. There was nothing I could do. I was trapped, locked inside a steel vessel with no escape.

Suddenly a woman two seats ahead of my husband unbuckled her seat belt and approached us. Crouching, she gave me a smile, extending her arms.

"May I?"

Embarrassed, I felt compelled to decline. Forcing a smile, I thanked her, offering false assurances that my daughter would soon be ok. She smiled again.

"Really, I don't mind. I work in our church nursery and I love holding babies."

When her arms reached for my baby, I did not protest. Tears of relief filled my eyes as she pulled my daughter to her chest, swaying her back and forth with hushing sounds. "I am a mother myself," she said. "I know how hard it can be. Get some rest. She will be fine." I could barely speak as my gratitude for this selfless stranger rendered me silent.

Though the memory had aged with my twins, the impression it left behind had not. I believe it is not until we witness an act of unexpected kindness or become the recipient of one that we become more aware of opportunities to reciprocate. An opportunity was before me now with the young mother and her two children, and I had a decision to make. I felt a stirring in my chest, an unsettling impulse to act while my brain played the role of devil's advocate. The easy route would be not to get involved, to ignore what was happening, and mind my own business. What if she refused?

What if I offended her?

The toddler screamed again, and the infant wailed. The man in front of me shook the pages of his opened newspaper while the stranger beside me put on headphones. I took a deep breath and unbuckled my seat belt.

My heart began beating faster, and my mouth went dry as I approached her seat. I knelt beside her, and our eyes met. Worry lines pinched her face and fear hid behind her eyes. I offered a smile; the same one I had received many years ago.

"May I?" I asked, my arms reaching out.

Her eyebrows shifted; confusion etched on her face. My presence caught the attention of her little girl. The toddler stuck a chubby finger into her wet mouth, looking up at me with tear-stained cheeks. Her big brown eyes were framed with the longest eyelashes I had ever seen. The mother bounced the wailing infant, her arms patting the back of the blanketed bundle while I waved at the little girl, then covered my eyes before quickly removing them with an expression of surprise. A wide, gummy smile revealed tiny buds of new teeth.

"May I?" I asked again, gesturing to the toddler's seat.

The mother said nothing but stood to let me in. My pulse raced as I reached for the little girl, half expecting her to screech at the stranger joining them. I looked different from her mother, with my blond hair and pale skin, but she climbed into my outstretched arms anyway. I pulled her onto my lap, relieved that she accepted me so readily. For the remainder of the flight, we entertained ourselves with games of "peekaboo" and "Itsy Bitsy Spider," but when the plane finally landed, something amazing happened. Nearby passengers suddenly sprang into action. Where the mother's earlier need for assistance with an overhead bag had been ignored, someone came forward and pulled it down for her. Another passenger asked if they could grab my bag. We exited the plane as a makeshift family, the toddler in my arms and the infant in hers, with strangers carrying our bags.

It felt complete, as though something had been fulfilled, a collective response to a silent call – one that didn't begin with me but with a stranger on a different plane several years ago, one who was willing to unbuckle her seatbelt and leave the confines of her comfort zone. Approaching a weary mother with two simple words.

"May I?"

By Brenda Watterson

17

Three Random Acts of Kindness Per Day

I was in line at Starbucks when I noticed the lady in the car behind me. Looking in my rearview mirror, I smiled as she tried to wrestle with impatient toddlers before ordering her coffee. She looked frustrated, and I thought to myself that she could use a little cheering up. I remembered our pastor's sermon on Sunday about showing random acts of kindness to strangers. He'd even passed out cards for us to give to strangers, to show God's love for them and to help brighten their day.

I thought to myself that I need to buy that woman's coffee. As I pulled up to the drive-through, I told the barista I would like to pay for the woman's coffee in the car behind me. He smiled and said, "That will be eight dollars and ten cents total, please." I gave him the money along with one of the cards from our church. I asked him to please give the card to the lady in the car behind me. He said with a smile on his face that he would gladly do so. I pulled off from the drive-through and watched the lady behind me as she pulled up to the line. I suddenly saw a huge smile break out on her face as she realized she did not have to pay for her coffee.

That made me feel good, and I hummed to myself as I drove to work. Once I got to work, I realized that I had blessed not only that lady but myself as well. Helping her made my day better also. I thought about what our pastor had said on Sunday at church, "by giving to others, we also give a gift to ourselves." I determined to practice what he had preached and began intentionally to bless at least three people per day. Once I got to work, I saw a coworker with her arms full.

She had her purse, some books, and her lunch box, and had a frazzled look on her face. I raced to the door to open it for her and let her in with a smile. I told her she looked lovely and to have a great day! She smiled in return and said, thank you. I continue to hum as I thought about the next person I could bless.

I continued these acts daily, and it was becoming a habit. I would compliment the lady at the gas station on her beautiful nails or nail polish color, the man behind me in the grocery line on his nice tie, or the waitress at the coffee shop on her interesting tattoo. I enjoyed seeing people and finding something beautiful to praise them for or ways to assist them. Sometimes it meant helping a single mom pay for her groceries, or sometimes it meant volunteering at the local mission, nursing home, or food kitchen. I often spent my weekends helping people who were elderly or disabled by doing yard work or giving their house a fresh coat of paint.

I started thinking to myself, 'What would happen if random acts of kindness became normal?' With that in mind, I went out every day looking to meet a need or even a want. I found out that kindness is more than just a good idea; it can be transformational. See a want? Meet a need! Every act of kindness can change someone's life positively.

Just like our pastor had told us, I found I could not out-give

God! The more I gave away, the more I received. What I gave away meant a lot to the people I gave to, but it gave me so much more. I loved loving and serving others!

I feel that the world would be a better place if we all performed acts of kindness at one time or another. The effects may be large or small, and their beneficiaries may not even be aware of them, but they can be profound, not only for the recipient but for the giver as well.

Performing three acts of kindness per day became a way of promoting love in the world and inspiring joy for myself and others. I found myself waking up every day, wondering what I could give away!

By Melanie Hardy

18

Punjabi Men, Very Strong

An opportunity was presented, which allowed me to see how kindness extended impacts those who observed it. I visited India for the first time two years ago. After touring the Lotus Temple in New Delhi, the Baha'i Faith House of Worship, and among the most inspiring architectural marvels of modern times, I proceeded to Punjab by train to visit the Golden Temple in Amritsar. The Golden Temple, by far one of the most serene temple grounds I've ever seen, is the sacred place of the Sikh religion. This impressive temple receives and feeds one hundred thousand people on average daily. After nine hours on the train, I arrived at Amritsar and checked into a family-owned hotel located 10 minutes' walking distance from the Golden Temple.

Traveling from New Delhi to Amritsar, Punjab by local train was quite an adventure. I wanted to experience 'real India' by taking a journey with the locals. The train door in coach class remained open throughout the trip, with passengers precariously hanging at the doors, some sitting on the floor, and the brave commuters relaxing on the roof of the train.

After spending two days in Amritsar touring, meditating, and enjoying exquisite Sikhs music at the Golden Temple, my next destination was Beas. It was time to visit the headquarters of the Radha Soami Satsang, a Surat Shabd Yoga spiritual tradition, located on the banks of the Beas River, in Punjab.

I brought my two carry-ons bags down the narrow staircase to the lobby of my hotel and requested a taxi to the bus station, where I would take a long-distance bus to the city of Beas, a journey of about 55 minutes. A slender young man who was hanging around the lobby rushed outside. I supposed he was the concierge. A few minutes later, he returned and announced that my taxi was waiting. I walked outside, looked around, and didn't see any taxi. All I saw was a thin, tall older man with a long white beard wearing a white kaftan with a matching white turban. He smiled at me but said nothing, and I was left confused. Sensing my confusion, the concierge intervened, "Sir, he is your taxi driver," pointing at the old man.

"Fine, but where is his taxi?" I asked.

He and the old man laughed as they showed me an antiquated cycle pedicab, also known as the rickshaw. "Is this some kind of a joke?" I thought to myself. The rickshaw, in my assessment, was not road worthy. Not only that, but the driver looked at least 80 years old.

"How far is the bus station?" I asked exasperated.

Again, they laughed, realizing I was underestimating both the cycle rickshaw and the driver.

"Only 15 to 20 minutes by taxi," replied the concierge with a smile.

"This man is going to ride this three-wheel bicycle with me sitting in the back with my luggage for 20 minutes?" I asked, growing more alarmed. At this point, the concierge proudly reassured me, "Sir, Punjabi men, very strong!" This brought a smile to the driver's face.

While I was busy conversing with the concierge and the driver, five women, each carrying a newborn baby, had surrounded me, begging for money. Looking into the eyes of the helpless and adorable babies, I couldn't resist putting a few rupees into the palm of each woman, which delighted them considerably.

After taking care of the beggars, our ride to the bus station began. The old man was rather impressive. He took off on the bike with the stamina of a young man, sometimes out-speeding motorists during a traffic jam. Then I noticed a hill in a short distance and worried how the old man would handle it. I was ready to get off the bike and help him push the pedicab up the hill. But to my amazement, the old man stood up from his seat, pedaling in a standing position, moaning and pedaling, and eventually made it up the hill, smiling and perspiring. Although I suspected it wasn't the first time he rode up the hill with a passenger, I was nonetheless concerned because I knew many men his junior couldn't handle the feat, let alone carry a passenger in the process.

When we got to the bus station, he pulled into the cycle rickshaw taxi area, where many other drivers were waiting for passengers. Having proudly completed his duty, he turned and looked at me with a smile, head tilted, with right hand outstretched for payment, "30 rupees, Sir." Other pedicab drivers and bystanders were watching curiously because, as a tourist, I stood out in India.

"No, I will not give you 30 rupees," I said, shaking my head.

There was a curious look in his eyes as he pulled a white

handkerchief from his shirt pocket to wipe off the beads of perspiration from his forehead.

"I will give you 100 rupees. That's what you deserve!" I said, appreciatively. A smile lit up the old man's face as he accepted my gift, rejoicing. And then something else happened. In just a few seconds, onlookers and other pedicab drivers were smiling and cheering as they witnessed a sudden burst of joyous excitement in the air, with the old man openly displaying his appreciation for the unexpected gift.

Kindness extended, received, and observed beneficially impact the feeling of everyone.

By Zeal Okogeri

Chapter Four

BE KIND
TO YOURSELF

A wise man does not chase
a black goat at night.

—African proverb

19

Gratitude for Human Kindness

Have you ever taken a journey on faith, without detailed plans, and in the end, it turned out to be a serendipitous adventure—appearing as though the entire trip was impeccably planned because, at every junction, you met generous and kind strangers who made you feel as if they'd been excitedly expecting you?

Mine was a soul-searching journey—a journey of self-discovery, to try to figure out who I am in my purest essence. With the encouragement of my Persian friend, I decided to pack and take a trip around the world the day after my graduation party. I had just completed my graduate studies in the history of art with a minor in archeology. I will share just a few of my experiences.

With my bags packed, I took off from my hometown of Stadl-Paura, Upper Austria, to my adventures. Soon after my arrival to New Zealand, I met a wonderful Swiss man, René, who took me on his motorbike to tour some of the most amazing parts of the country, such as Punakaiki, a village in the South Island known for the natural wonders of the Paparoa National Park, sandy beaches, rocky coastlines, and many lush subtropical rainforest, rivers, and spectacular mountains. Then off to Christchurch, the largest city in the South Island of New Zealand known for its English heritage, and Queenstown, renowned for adventure sports! Queenstown's most famous thrill-seeking activity is bungee jumping. All over New Zealand, you can jump from bridges, the edge of cliffs, and stadium roofs. Since I was on a journey of self-discovery, it was time to liberate myself by letting go of some of my fears; so, I took the plunge! Bungee jumping is not for the faint-hearted, but it is an experience that one never forgets. As if bungee jumping was not enough, I went for another adventure, skydiving! It was my first parachute jump! The heart-stopping adrenalin and adventure of skydiving aren't easy to describe. It must be experienced—not that I'm necessarily recommending it. But once I overcame the initial fear of being at 15,000 feet in the air and plummeting toward the ground at 125 miles per hour, there was a sense of freedom that I never felt before as I soared over the most dramatic scenery in New Zealand, free-falling over lakes and snow-capped mountains. It was during this experience that I realized the degree to which I had allowed fear to hold me back.

In Melbourne, Australia, I dropped into a beautiful small coffee shop to ask for directions. I ended up with another private tour guide who drove me in his vintage Mustang to the best places to visit, including a ride along the Great Ocean Road, the world-famous stretch of the Australian coastline. If that wasn't enough generosity, one of the owners of the coffee shop gifted me his downtown apartment to stay for the rest of my journey in Melbourne.

In the United States, I spent several months in a blockhouse in Maine with my gracious host, Klaus, one of my best friends from back home, who owns a sea and land plane company. Here, the living was 'back to nature,' with gardening, swimming in natural springs, deer and moose sightings, driving a pickup truck along dead-end roads, and flying up to camp in "nowhere land."

As people kept popping into my life, my journey continued to Dubai, the Solomon Islands in the southeast of Papua New Guinea, and to Brisbane Australia.

In Brisbane, a generous family invited a friend and me to stay with them until we got settled because we decided to live in Australia for a while. We had a fine time being together, except for one problem. It was during this time that a big flood hit Brisbane. It rained for almost two months straight. Although our home was fine because it was built on a high elevation, other homes, shops, and supermarkets were not okay. As a result, there was a severe shortage of food and water. We had to keep water in the bathtubs because the supermarkets had run out entirely. Almost no food was available, either! Fortunately, we could buy food in a fresh market. But nothing could dull our joy for the kindness and generosities we received.

After almost five years of traveling around the world, my last destination was Singapore. It is here that I had the pleasure of meeting a beautiful soul, Dr. Zeal, at a spiritual community gathering. Our friendship culminated in my being a part of this heart-warming book on kindness and compassion. After my time in Singapore, I moved back to Vienna, this time for good, to follow up on my university studies, lecturing in art history and philosophy, and working in one of the largest privately held museum for contemporary art in Austria. I now have a lovely daughter who has turned my life around in the most beautiful way. She is a real gem and I am looking forward to traveling with her soon!

My journey around the world not only liberated me significantly, but it also reaffirmed my faith in human kindness, compassion, and generosity. Despite the negative news we read in the newspapers and see on television every day, there are still a lot of good, decent, and kind-hearted people out there! Since my journey, I've been encouraging others to embrace the world. I tell people to carry a smile on their lips and travel, and if they don't speak the language of the country they're visiting or know what the correct behavior should be, they should listen inwardly and go with the flow. Everything will be fine.

Having the courage to leave your familiar surroundings to broaden your horizons and experience nature's boundless beauty, wonders, and generosities can be one of the greatest gifts you can ever give yourself.

By Marlene Elvira Steinz

20

Transforming Our Flaws into Gifts

There was a Water Bearer who had two large pots. Each hung on the end of a pole which he carried across his neck. One of the pots had a crack in it. While the other pot was perfect and always delivered a full portion of water at the end of the long walk from the stream to the master's house, the cracked pot arrived only half full. For a full two years, this went on daily, with the bearer delivering only one and one-half pots of water to his master's house.

The perfect pot was proud of its accomplishments, perfect to the end for which it was made. But the poor cracked pot was ashamed of its imperfection and miserable that it could accomplish only half of what it had been made to do. After two years of what it perceived to be a bitter failure, it spoke to the Water Bearer one day by the stream. "I am ashamed of myself, and I want to apologize to you."

"Why?" asked the bearer. "What are you ashamed of?" "I have been able, for these past two years, to deliver only half my load because this crack in my side causes water to leak out all the way back to your master's house. Because of my flaws, you must do all of this work, and you don't get full value from your efforts," the pot said.

The Water Bearer felt sorry for the old cracked pot. In his compassion, he said, "As we return to the master's house, I want you to notice the beautiful flowers along the path." Indeed, as they went up the hill, the old cracked pot took notice of the sun warming the beautiful wildflowers on the side of the path, and this cheered it some. But at the end of the trail, it still felt bad because it had leaked out half its load, and so again, it apologized to the bearer for its failure.

The bearer said to the pot, "Did you notice that there were flowers on your side of your path, but not on the other pot's side? That's because I have always known about your flaw, and I took advantage of it. I planted flower seeds on your side of the path, and every day while we walk back from the stream, you've watered them. For two years, I have been able to pick these beautiful flowers to decorate my master's table. Without you being just the way you are, he would not have this beauty to grace his house."

Each of us has his and her unique flaws. We are all cracked pots. But if we will allow it, the Divine will use our flaws to grace others' paths. In God's great economy, nothing goes to waste. So, as you go through life and serve in your best and highest capacity, don't be afraid of your flaws. Acknowledge them and allow the Divine to take advantage of them; you, too, can be the cause of beauty in life. Go out boldly, knowing that in our weakness, we can find strength, and with God, all things are possible.

By Anonymous

21

If You Do Not Take Care of Your Body, Where Do You Plan to Live?

I was given the rare opportunity to witness the devastating effects of cigarette smoking while interning at the University Health Center in Pasadena, near Los Angeles. I had rented a room in a large house owned by a couple in their 60s. When I finalized the rental agreement with the lady, her husband was not there. I asked about him, and she said he was in the hospital. She said nothing further. I was reluctant to ask more questions because I could see from the pained expression on her face that she didn't want to talk about it.

When I returned from work the following day, I saw her sitting at the kitchen table, looking worried. I asked if she was all right. It was at this point that she brought out the family photo album and started showing me photos of her and her husband. They had been a "high-society" couple. The album was filled with photographs of them in the company of famous politicians, movie stars, and international celebrities. It was evident from the pictures that they had once been an active couple and had plenty of good times together.

Remorsefully, she said her husband had smoked cigarettes for 30 years and was dying of lung cancer in the hospital. "The fool won't stop smoking," she lamented. "He'll be coming home in a couple of days to stay for a few weeks before returning to the hospital."

Before long, a hospital aide brought the man home and wheeled him to his room, which was next to mine. He was hooked up to an oxygen tank and used a walker to support his weight. His bathroom was right across the hall from his room. It took the man at least 10 minutes to get from his room to the bathroom. He ran out of breath after taking only two steps and had to wait a while to recuperate before taking another step.

It was a painful sight to watch this man with an oxygen tube trailing behind him as he struggled to make it across the hallway. On occasion, he was unable to make it in time and wet his trousers. He couldn't sleep at night because he had extreme difficulty breathing. I couldn't sleep either, for I could hear him struggling to breathe. After a few days, his condition grew worse. He was taken back to the hospital, where he died peacefully.

He had created a lot of suffering, not only for himself but also for his family; his death came as a great relief to them. During the last five years of his life with metastatic lung cancer, his family had been working around the clock to take care of him. One person would buy oxygen; another would pick him up from the hospital, another would cook for him, bathe him, etc. In a sense, his complete dependence on other people became a burden to his family. It was also a source of unimaginable pain to the man who was once a vibrant and independent person.

This was an eye-opening experience, and I wished everyone who is currently battling with nicotine addiction, especially young people, had the opportunity to see the devastating effects of long-term cigarette smoking. When we are young, our youthful exuberance deceives us into thinking we are invincible, that nothing can happen to us. We continue to beat up the body until it just can't take it anymore.

A wise person once remarked, "If you do not take care of your body, where do you plan to live?" As we get older, we realize that we need to be kinder to ourselves by taking the best care of our bodies. It's the only one we have, and we want it to go as far as it can in a healthy state, so that we can live in it comfortably. We learn to exercise, eat the right foods, take nutritional supplements, get regular medical checkups, and preventative care, and to resist anything that would bring about ailments.

Being sick sucks! It takes the fun out of life. Instead of living an exciting life and trying to materialize your dreams, you'll find yourself preoccupied with worrying about your health, visiting emergency rooms, keeping up with your doctors' appointments, and making sure you take your medications on time.

Most ailments are preventable through self-vigilance and lifestyle modifications. Unfortunately, when we are young, many of us don't have the awareness that it is our number one priority to take care of ourselves.

If we want to help others by practicing kindness, we must realize that before we can help anyone else, we must first be viable. Perhaps you've heard this announcement in the airplane: "In the unlikely event of a sudden loss in cabin pressure, oxygen masks will deploy from the ceiling compartment located above you. <u>Secure your own oxygen mask first</u> before helping others."

There's a very good reason for taking care of yourself first.

By Zeal Okogeri

22

Simple Acts of Kindness Changed My Life

Josh wanted so much to be accepted in school. He wanted to socialize with other students and engage in simple activities like playing basketball or sitting with a group, sharing stories, and laughing. Instead, he was frequently bullied by his classmates. He tried every means to deal with the bullying issue effectively, but nothing worked.

Josh was growing tired of being a target of bullying and a nobody. He knew there were better things in life for him than continuously reacting to bullies. He was tired of feeling tense, anxious, and frustrated. He was tired of increasingly developing low self-esteem and losing his confidence.

As a last resort, he decided to start over by moving to another school. From day one, he adopted a new attitude and approach, which he hoped would help him get along with his fellow students. Determined not to be bullied again, he took charge and began demonstrating the opposite of bullying—kindness. His goal was to show that he cares. He hoped that people would start caring a bit more for each other and take care of each other through his example. Little did Josh know to what extent he was going to transform the school.

His relentless acts of kindness became noticed, then caught on throughout the school.

"It's possible to turn any situation around. Even though I was scared, I took the jump."

The 'jump' Josh refers to, was having the courage to leave an unsupportive environment, his previous school, and adopting a new attitude toward others. Now, instead of expecting to be bullied and trying to deal with the situation, he chose to take charge. He would reach out to his fellow students, speaking with them before they approached him. "I wanted to reach out to people and show them who I was, and I knew I had to take action, no matter how small. I guess amazing things happen when you believe in yourself," Josh would say.

What was this one thing that changed Josh's life and inspired so many students to give kindness a try?

Every morning, Josh arrived early at school. He stood at the main entrance and opened the door as students arrived, cheerfully greeting each person, "Good morning." His devotion to duty was admirable. Through the ripple effect of kindness, other students began to demonstrate kindness in their own unique ways.

It's empowering and heartwarming to watch kindness spread. Opening doors gives people hope. It tells them someone cares. People got to know Josh, and he got to know many of the students. Soon, Josh regained his self-confidence and looked forward to going to school every day.

One student commented on the transformation Josh brought to the school, "It changed the way I thought about things and the way

I felt about myself."

Kindness is love in action and love always wins.

How can we demonstrate kindness in our lives?

Well, here are some ideas. If these don't touch your life, perhaps, they can be the catalyst for other ideas that will:

We can find unique ways to surprise people in our lives. How about baking some cookies to share with co-workers? Tell them they are appreciated, especially if they've been supportive.

We can be courteous by stepping aside and letting someone in a hurry or a person with a disability go through the supermarket checkout before us. We can offer our seat on the bus to an older person.

We can offer encouragement to our teammates in sporting events, telling them that they are doing a great job. We can praise friends for their accomplishments and give them words of encouragement and support.

We can be thoughtful and give to the homeless. When we're out shopping, we can collect a few things like a toothbrush, toothpaste, or deodorant, and give to the homeless. Maybe we can offer a meal as well.

It's up to each of us how we choose to show kindness. Kindness has changed my life and the lives of so many others. It has the power to transform any situation.

One lady emailed me yesterday. She said she almost died three times in the last seven months, but she's been able to laugh and smile because of the kindness message we've been spreading. She learned to be kind to her nurses and doctors, which resulted in them treating her with more kindness. In fact, they look forward to going to her room in the hospital because of her positive spirit, thoughtfulness, and gratitude.

I believe the world needs more kindness. But we also need to be kind to ourselves. This is one area that some people struggle with the most, yet it's the most crucial area because our lives depend on it.

During a recent interview, I was asked how I can measure the impact of my acts of kindness so far.

My answer was simple: "I can't!"

"You can't measure the impact of a kind act because its reach is far greater than we can imagine."

By Andreas Jones

23

Be Willing
to Ask for Help

I was taking a walk one Sunday afternoon at the park in Mission Beach, San Diego, when I noticed a group of homeless people. "Everyone has a story," I thought. I wondered how some of these people, now in their 40s, 50s, and 60s, became homeless. I decided to have a conversation with one of them. "Bob" had come to San Diego from North Carolina. He was about 48 years old. He had been in the landscaping business in North Carolina for several years but got laid off. Not having any other marketable skills, he did odd jobs to support himself. Unfortunately, everything he did fell apart. He went from one failure to the next until he was no longer able to pay his bills. Instead of going back home to live with his parents or asking friends for a loan, Bob decided to leave town. He wanted to escape the embarrassment and humiliation of being jobless and homeless, where people knew him.

He hitchhiked to San Diego, arriving with no money, and

saw no alternative but to join the homeless living in the park until he figured out what to do next. Bob was different from many other homeless people because he didn't try to escape reality by drinking, smoking, or using drugs. He exercised regularly by riding his bicycle to the public library, where he read newspapers and kept abreast of current events. I asked Bob if his family knew of his whereabouts. He said no. I asked if his family would help him out if they knew of his predicament. "Yes," he said. His mother had just remarried, and her new husband was well off. Then he sighed, looked shamefully to the ground, and said, "I guess I'm too proud to ask her and her husband for money."

I asked him if he had a family of his own. He said no that he had never been married. "If I can't even support myself," he said, "what sense would it make trying to support someone else?"

I asked him to share with me some of the challenges of being homeless.

He said that he tries to stay out of the public eye. "People don't like us homeless, so I try to stay out of their sight. At first, it hurt my feelings, but I've gotten over it. The other thing that's a real problem is the rain. When it rains, it's hard to find a dry spot. So, I cover myself up with plastic, and that usually keeps me dry and warm. I also have to make a hole in the plastic so I can breathe." Then he added, "I'm grateful, though, because we get one free meal per day, and I get to enjoy the ocean view and the beautiful San Diego weather. Yes, it gets lonely sometimes because you have no money to do things and no one to do things with. And when you look around, you see everyone having fun, and you just feel so lonely."

With that, I encouraged him to consider calling his family to let them know of his circumstances. "Sometimes, when we are so deep in the water and unable to swim any longer, it takes a lifeline to get us to the surface," I said. "There's nothing wrong with asking for help as long we do not make a habit of leaning on others. We all need to pull our weight."

He then asked me about my story. I asked him how much time he had. Wrong question! He had all day. After a summary of my life story, which seemed to delight and cheer him up a bit, we thanked each other for the opportunity to share and learn from each other.

Although I walked many times again in the park at Mission Beach, I never saw Bob again. I like to think he called his family and accepted their help to come home or at least find better circumstances.

By Zeal Okogeri

24

The Missing Peace

K indness can shape our world and our perspective toward other living beings. It can give us a sense of purpose in life. When we are treated kindly, we receive a sense of belonging and the belief that we exist to feel joy and happiness. Even plants are believed to grow faster, stronger, and healthier when spoken to kindly. It's something a lot of us, if not every living being, have an insatiable thirst for, and the opportunities can come in many different forms by humans and non-humans alike. The opposite is true as well. Without kindness, the world and life can appear to be a cold place filled with constant struggles and challenges.

Growing up in an authoritarian household for a good part of my childhood, frequently changing schools, and dealing with bullies, I never really felt I belonged anywhere. My only escape became my grandparent's house, where their dog, Clover, resided. She was my only real friend and the only being that loved me unconditionally. When she passed away unexpectedly during my early years in high school, my heart shattered. Several years later, when my aunty (and mentor) also passed away, the little hope I had for a bright future became dim and buried under an avalanche of despair. I thought about moving to another country and starting a new path in life. I considered joining a monastery; after all, what better source to turn to for peace in my life? A month after the funeral, however, destiny took me on a detour. I found myself moving back to the island of Oahu and in with my mother and four new roommates whom she had adopted a few years earlier.

Being the type of person who never liked to move backward in life, I resented this new road that Fate had me traveling. Moreover, I had never had cats before and was a bit annoyed when her youngest, a Maine Coon named Valentine, followed me around the house from the first day. "Don't you want to play with your brothers?" I'd ask him as I carried him out of my room for the fifth time in one day. But all he would do was meow to me and nuzzle my cheek as I sat him down in the living room. I couldn't help but wonder what this little feline's motive was. I did my best to keep an emotional distance from him, but every morning for several weeks, he would stretch his paw under the door and meow until I let him into my room. Each time this occurred, I couldn't help but be amazed at his reason for entering my room.

As I climbed back into bed, he gingerly walked onto my chest, laid his head against my heart, and purred contentedly. When I opened my eyes and saw this little cat, seemingly so happy to be near me, it gave me the warmest feeling of belonging. On two occasions over the next year, I underwent dental surgery and came down with a severe case of the flu. During those times, Valentine rarely left my side, keeping me warm by leaning his head on my pillow. Not long after that, during a routine visit to the vet, he was diagnosed with kidney failure, requiring several days of hospitalization. I accepted the news with little reaction, but my mornings following that were not the same without his soft purrs, and his body curled up next to me. I felt a missing piece in my heart without him by my side. The next day I set up a visitation with him at the vet clinic and nervously followed the technician down the hallway, unsure of what to expect. As I turned the corner into the room, he stood up to greet me. My eyes drifted over to the I.V. pole hooked up to his catheter, and suddenly I broke down. It was as if he understood how much I was hurting inside, for he remained still as I hugged him tightly until my cries turned into hiccups, and his fur became thoroughly drenched with my tears. Everything in our relationship and my heart changed from that day forward.

My heart began to heal, wanting to reciprocate the kindness he had shown to me from the start. Despite my fear of needles, I learned to administer medication to him and to provide at-home fluid treatments. Over time my instincts became more sensitive to the point where I even detected a tumor before his doctor discovered it. Despite his rollercoaster ride with kidney cancer, Valentine enjoyed an additional five years, attributed to his fierce willpower for life. He is my hero and was a positive example for other cats and their pet parents to opt for treatment to extend their lives and quality of life. His kindness was not just a lighthouse for my lost soul but for other animals as well, and now when I look into the eyes of my next generation of adopted pets, I see the same kindness and compassion he always displayed. It's a service that I've learned is a reciprocated act, regardless of species. I am forever grateful to my young cat who healed my heart. Although he was taken far too soon, I've been reassured, through the help of an intuitive healer, that he is being well taken care of and is content.

By Stacey Shimabukuro

25

Kindness is Letting Go of Grudges

Hello, reader. I beg your pardon; I haven't done this before, ever. I am new to speaking one on one with people on paper. Oh, I can see by the look on your face that you are a bit confused. Please, let me explain. You see, I am not actually Beverly, the author of this story. I am Beverly's grudge.

You see, when you hold a grudge for a long time, the grudge can take over. It can consume the individual exactly as I did with Beverly. But let me digress a bit, please; let me first explain what a grudge is. A grudge is a feeling of ill will, resentment, anger, and even hate. Beverly and her brother Junie had been holding a grudge against each other for over 20 years!

Beverly and Junie were not always enemies. In fact, they grew up very close as a brother and sister should. One time, Junie saved Beverly's life when she was drowning. He pulled her out of the pool. She was five, and he was seven.

After that, they were as thick as thieves; you didn't see one without the other. They grew up as best friends.

That all changed when Junie was drafted into the military and sent to fight in Vietnam. When he came back, he was a different man. He was now angry and argumentative. He and Beverly fought all the time. One day, he said something to Beverly that made her so mad that she vowed never to speak to him again. That's when I came into the picture because a grudge loves it when you make a vow like that. I knew I was in it for the long run. It was so warm and cozy inside Beverly, where I had a front-row seat to all the fighting and arguing.

The grudge between the two continued to escalate, and even their families were involved. Their children started forming grudges of their own. Now, that's precisely what a grudge lives for!

But alas, I had interference from their mother, who would show up unexpectedly and confront Beverly with things like, "What are you doing?" "This has gone on for too long." "This is not how you two were raised!" And after every scolding by the mother, I felt my presence shrink.

Luckily for me, the mother became ill. She was hospitalized. And a wonderful thing occurred (for me, that is). Beverly and her brother were arguing in the hospital room. That moment was glorious to a grudge like me!

Not long after that, the mother passed away. So sad! But not for me, for you see, this was a grudge's opportunity to poison even more family members at the funeral. But all of a sudden, I could not move. I was frozen to one spot and unable to spread even one more malice. I looked at the doors to the chapel just as they swung open, and guess who came sashaying into the service? LOVE. That's right, LOVE. You see, I had been on Beverly's back as her grudge for 20 years, but her mother had LOVE in her heart for her entire life. LOVE swept in and filled the whole room, touching everyone's heart.

After that, Beverly and Junie began to talk. They went out to brunch and spent time at each other's homes. Their children came together, and they spent their first Christmas together in years. Now they are planning a family reunion.

Hello, this is the real Beverly, not the grudge. The grudge is gone. My brother Junie and I are working hard on becoming friends again. It feels good. Our only regret is that we had to lose our mother to see how important family is and how family and love go hand in hand. The author William Arthur Ward once said, "A life lived without forgiveness is a prison." And in the words of Martin Luther King, Jr. "It's never too late to do what's right."

Junie and I are finally doing what's right, thanks to love and forgiveness.

By Beverly Peace-Kayhill

26

Kindness is a Gift

Kindness is a gift. It can happen by chance. It is like an umbrella on a rainy day—sometimes quite literally—as when a random stranger on the sidewalk offered me an umbrella during an unexpected downpour. I was one among many scrambling on a crowded sidewalk in New York's fashionable SoHo neighborhood when the sunny sky was rapidly replaced by a blanket of ominous dark blue-grey clouds. When the rain began, people began to disperse – some taking shelter in stores, others in cafes, and a few running. I wonder if I was offered the umbrella because this kind stranger had seen me attempt to do the impossible: walk in between the rain drops by ducking under the awning or scaffold.

Kindness is energizing. Once a customer in front of me in line at an airport coffee shop picked up the bill for my tea. Her offering to pay it forward probably gave me more energy than did the caffeine in my hot beverage of choice.

Kindness is good for the economy. I try to bank kindness by paying it forward. If I know a friend might be alone for a holiday, I invite them to join my family – knowing that I, too, may be in their shoes one day.

Kindness is spontaneity. We spring into action without

thinking when we see someone in need of help. I invited an elderly Scottish couple into a coffee shop and paid for their tea after the wife nearly collapsed from exhaustion after sightseeing on a hot, humid summer day.

Kindness is responsibility. A server at a restaurant accidentally knocked an entire glass of red wine onto my white cashmere sweater, which I had recently received for my birthday. I needed to change out of my clothes and the restaurant directed me to a store a couple doors down. My new friend at lunch came with me and consoled me. The store's staff was quite helpful. When we came back to the restaurant, they gave us the best table and offered us lunch on the house. They took my stained clothes to be cleaned and later reimbursed me the cost of the clothing that couldn't be cleaned.

Kindness is good citizenship. I came to the immediate assistance of an elderly man who had been knocked out cold upon suffering a blunt hit to his head from a man with a clear garbage bag full of recycled bottles. I got help; he survived the blow and healed.

Kindness provides housing. I needed a new place to stay when I was studying in London. The lease on my temporary rental was finished and my flatmate had other plans. I was passing through France and mentioned this to my best friend's mother. She immediately offered to let me stay with them, as she and her husband were being transferred to London. Though their daughter stayed in Paris for her studies, I stayed the entire semester in a beautiful residential enclave of Swiss Cottage rent free on the second floor of their duplex. I reciprocated the generosity through presents and by keeping my friend's mother company after classes, particularly when her husband traveled for business.

Kindness is community. I was sitting at my desk at work when my sister called and said, "Mom is dead." I shrieked and started to cry. One of my colleagues came up to me with an offering of a tissue. I decided to go home. Two of my colleagues, Barbara and Beth, decided that they should drive me home instead of me driving myself. One drove in my car and the other followed so that they would both have a way back to the office. It was very thoughtful of them. My mother's death was an unexpected one. She had died as a result of an accident. Soon after, my sister and I arranged our mother's memorial service and burial. Without much time to spare, I traveled across the country to clean out my mom's rental apartment. It was going to be a daunting experience. I flew from New York to Los Angeles via Denver. When I was waiting at the gate, I noticed a jolly group of people traveling together. They were heading to some music festival I had never heard of. They were genuinely empathic when I answered their question about why I was traveling. They prayed for me. I was a little taken aback at their very public display. It isn't something we see in the Northeast, though I kept that thought to myself and received their prayer with the same authenticity in which it was offered.

Kindness is most noticeable to both the giver and receiver when the benefactor is in real need. I arrived in California in the pitch black of the night and picked up the rental car to drive to my hotel. The car didn't have a GPS system and I had printed out my directions. For reasons unknown to me, suddenly I could barely read them. I always had good eyesight and was just starting to wear readers but I didn't have them with me. I found my way, but not without getting a little lost and having to ask for directions from strangers in the parking lot of a restaurant. I wasn't necessarily in the safest place, yet the strangers really helped me out. The next day, one of my mother's church friends picked me up at my hotel and brought me to my mother's apartment. I wasn't too keen on driving around – or at least not alone – so we took turns. It was quite the project to clean out her apartment in a limited amount of time. I didn't have the luxury of putting it all into storage and dealing with it later.

My brother-in-law, Wayne, came in from Portland to help me for one day. His kindness brought him luck. He had been looking for a vintage car, a Thunderbird. Interestingly, there was a vintage Thunderbird in the vicinity and he ended up buying it. My Uncle Peter came in from Denver. Jan, a lifelong friend of my mother's from college, came from Nevada and a group of Mother's friends from church came. I gave away almost everything to her friends and various charities. I brought back a few things of sentimental value for my sister and me.

After reflecting on how I've benefited from kindness, I know that kindness is also togetherness. We have no knowledge of why we are here and what life's purpose is, yet I do know that we do it better when we share life's sorrows and joys.

By Noelle Newell

27

The Kindness Project

I teach the high-ability section of third grade students at my school. By the time they reach me, many of them have been together in the same class since kindergarten. They grow very close and, in many cases, behave a lot like siblings. This can be a very special relationship for kids to share – growing and changing together, making many memories along the way. It can also be tough when someone is unhappy and their reactions aren't as guarded as they would be in newer relationships. We always seem to hurt the ones we are closest to, knowing they will still be around even if you say something upsetting.

Last year, there seemed to be a bit more girl drama than usual. I also had a mix of boys who could be harsh with each other at times. I didn't like the social/emotional road we seemed to be driving on. Feelings were getting hurt on a regular basis, students were taking advantage of others' weaknesses, and I felt like the kids weren't happy with each other. I dreaded the stories I would hear when they came back from recess each day. "Becca said she's only playing with Hailey." "Max wouldn't share the ball with us." "Tori's mom said she can't play with Zane anymore and Zane tried to play with her anyway."

I often launch discussions and class meetings with books so I can relate what I want to talk about with characters and their situations. I read the story Coasting Casey to the kids. Casey gets into some trouble for not working hard in class, for drawing on his desk, and for not paying attention. We made a list of all the traits in Casey that needed improvement.

In my classroom, when we recognize something we need to do better, we call it a growth spurt. Growth spurts help us learn from our mistakes or poor choices to be successful and meet goals. (My kids are constantly setting goals for their academic life and for social and emotional development.)

After focusing on Casey's possible growth spurts, we looked at all his positive traits. He is creative, he can play musical instruments, and he's a gifted artist. We discussed some of the reasons Casey may have been having trouble at school. Then we discussed some of our own positive traits and some of the things we need to work on. We discovered every one of us has strengths and qualities that make us special and every one of us has things we can work on.

I bought a box of nine-by-six manila envelopes and introduced a kindness project. Each day, whoever the student of the day was would be the student we really paid attention to for the day. We tried to spend extra time with him/her, talk to him/her, study him/her, notice things about him/her. Then, at the end of the day, the student of the day got an envelope to decorate while the rest of the class each got a half sheet of paper to write a few sentences with positive traits about that person. We would open our envelopes on World Kindness Day, November 13.

We talked about how to write "thoughtful" sentences about the person. They couldn't just say, "He's nice" or "She is fun." They had to really be specific and sincere. This caused a couple of things to happen. When it was someone's turn to be student of the day, he knew he was being watched carefully by his classmates. He knew kids were going to be looking for the good things about him and wanted to be sure there were positive things to write about. It really made the kids stop and think about their behavior and actions toward others.

This continued through the whole class roster. Each student of the day became a rock star in the class and tried to put his best foot forward. Students who originally clashed with other students now had to come up with only positive things to say about them. While the students were writing their good thoughts, I took the time to write about each student as well.

When we were finished each day, we placed our pages in the decorated envelope with the child's name on it. (After school, I proofread them all to be sure there were no vague or negative comments.) I kept all the sealed envelopes in a special place until every student had been the student of the day.

The students were counting down the days until they could open their special envelopes. Almost every day, I heard, "Can we please just peek in our envelopes?" or "Can't the kids who are done read theirs?"

I wish I had recorded their reactions the day I passed them out. It was better than any Christmas morning, better than any birthday party. They wiggled in their seats, hardly able to contain themselves in anticipation. They couldn't wait to read the positive comments from their classmates.

"Are they all passed out yet?"

"Can we open them now?"

This is another reminder that positive affirmation and acceptance trump any kind of material reward or gift. They yearned for praise from their peers. When I gave them the green light, they tore into the envelopes and devoured each note.

One by one, faces lit up, smiles abounded, a few kids ran over to hug other kids, and there were even some happy tears. They didn't want to put them away. They read and reread their notes and beamed with excitement. I heard a very artistic girl in the class say, "Everyone thinks I'm good at drawing!" It seemed so obvious to everyone but her. The boy known to bully others couldn't hold back his smile, perhaps feeling accepted for the first time in a long while. I had forgotten to write to one of the students and she pointed it out right away. Many of them had sought out my note first to see what I had written. I heard one surprised student exclaim, "Mrs. Anderson wrote about us too?!"

The important message I wanted the kids to internalize was that every person in the room was special and had positive traits. Every person deserves to be valued and cared about. We may not agree with the choices someone makes in a situation, but if we can talk to the person with compassion, we can do more than co-exist in the room. We can help each other grow and work together to make improvements.

Of course, the other benefit to this project was to boost the confidence of those students who may not have believed in themselves. Sometimes a student will feel like someone doesn't like him/her, but when they read positive thoughts from that person, that student knows they are admired for something.

I wanted to continue to do something to spread kindness throughout the year so that my students would be reminded to look for the good in others. We started a Kindness Tree in the main hallway of our school. We shared our idea with all classrooms; whenever someone sees an act of kindness, they can write it on a heart-shaped leaf and give it to the student to staple on the tree. Our Kindness Tree is a daily reminder that kindness matters. It warms my heart when I have a student come up and ask, "Can I fill out a kindness heart for Audrey? She shared her change at the book fair so I could get the book I wanted." Or "Kyla asked me to play at recess when she saw me sitting on the Buddy Bench." (This is a bench on the playground you can sit on when you can't find a buddy to play with.)

Another opportunity to promote kindness is Random Acts of Kindness Day on February 17. I have my students participate by coming up with ways to make someone's day in the school. We focus on all school personnel. We have made appreciation cards for the cooks, librarian, custodians, etc. We have also collected donations of fun Post-its, candy, fuzzy socks, colorful pens, etc. for the teachers in the school.

When I talk to my students from last year, they tell me they saved their envelopes. It is something they turn to on bad days to remember the positive things their classmates said about them. Some of the teachers and school personnel we gave inspirational cards and signs to still have them hanging up. The Kindness Tree is ever-blooming with praise on heart-shaped leaves. I truly believe that performing all these intentional acts of kindness and teaching compassion to our students goes a long way. It seems like we often focus on an anti-bullying curriculum, but I like the positive slant of always seeking ways to be kind and encouraging to others.

By Shannon Anderson

28

Curvy Kindness

I found the 28-day challenge one day while scrolling through social media shared by a friend. The post was colorful and caught my attention, challenging anyone who dared to give up 'bad' foods like processed foods containing preservatives and sugars, fast food, and any sort of white bread or pasta for 28 days. The challenge advertised weight loss results and improved energy.

"Boy, wouldn't that be nice?" I thought.

I'm a curvy woman. Prominent hips and a rump are a family trait. I've always struggled with having confidence in my appearance, a war that intensified in my brain after pregnancy. I'm not traditionally what folks may call skinny, but my body is proportionate, and I know what to wear to complement my hills and valleys.

My energy level bothered me more than my appearance. Married, with three kids, and each one in an after-school activity, and with two ferrets and three cats, my life was a whirlwind of running here, there, and everywhere. I was barely 30 years old and knew I should not be this tired all the time at my age. I could feel in my soul that I was not being kind to myself, and I sensed that the negativity I directed at myself could also be an energy drain. There didn't seem to be enough coffee in the world to keep me energized and awake. I had enough of yawning my way through the whole day and hating my looks. So, I took up the 28-day challenge to show my body and my soul some much overdue love.

I started in January just after New Year's as my resolution. The week before, I cooked up what was left of the 'bad' food in our house. On my next grocery trip, I hit the unfamiliar organic selections in every aisle of the grocery store. I cut out fast food and began to carry organic granola bars and apples in my purse instead. I bought fresh fruits and vegetables; grain-fed, antibiotic-free proteins; and sugar-free, whole-grain bread.

Since I do most of the grocery shopping, that meant the entire family would take the challenge too. I knew I would fail if tempted by any easy-to-cook, processed foods, or sweets left in the house. My family's objections lasted only a short while. After tasting my freshly cooked meals made with real, all-natural food, they began to request healthier food for dinner. "Mom, please make that crock-pot chicken with carrots and rice" became music to my ears.

Our new food was rich with depth of flavor. I still ate spaghetti; I just made it with whole-grain noodles, real spices, and roasted tomato sauce. There was never a piece left of my whole-wheat garlic bread made with organic butter—a favorite of my first grader. I ate turkey and avocado sandwiches with an organic dressing. We made chips and salsa, stir fry, and even pizza on flaxseed dough. We were all still enjoying the same dishes we had always enjoyed, just made with organic, all-natural, and sugar-free ingredients. None of this food tasted like diet food as I had feared. It tasted different, though. It tasted bright and better than the food I prepared before.

After two weeks of avoiding bad food and learning about good foods, I found myself waking up with a little more bounce in my step in the mornings, but also having strong cravings. I slipped and ate a bag of chocolate-covered peanuts offered by a coworker. I did not beat myself up over it and instead opted for forgiveness, remembering to stay kind to myself.

Around the twenty-first day of the challenge, I noticed my pants fitting a bit looser. I weighed myself and, sure enough, eight pounds had melted away. I felt lighter and younger. I had energy. I was getting more chores done around the house. I was not yawning all day and drank less coffee. My kids said they missed some of their favorites of our old food, but that they too were generally feeling better and more awake throughout the day.

"We've got to keep going! Imagine how you will feel after 28 days," I encouraged them.

On the twenty-eighth day of the challenge, my spouse and I decided we never wanted to go back to feeling so drained as we did before the challenge. We now had several meals figured out that were easy to prepare, healthy, and delicious. We are getting used to the organic brands and have learned how to check labels for chemicals and sugars. We decided to make the challenge our new way of life. Over a year has passed since we took the challenge. I am down 30 pounds. I love my curves, and I am more confident now than before. The weight loss is great, but what I'm happiest about is how amazing and healthy I feel after learning to be kinder to myself.

By Mary Anglin-Coulter

29

Be True to Yourself

There's a story about a woman whose son was addicted to sugar. She tried everything to stop this young boy from consuming so much sugar, but nothing worked. Finally, her friends encouraged her to take her son to see a respected wise man—Mahatma Gandhi.

But she pondered how she could arrange an audience with such a great man. Fortunately, after contacting Gandhi's assistant, with the help of friends, the wise man agreed to see the woman and her son.

Kneeling before Gandhi, she pleaded with him to persuade her stubborn son to stop eating sugar.

Gandhi didn't answer her for a few moments. Then he told her to bring her son back in two weeks. The woman agreed with excitement and couldn't wait to return.

Two weeks later, the woman, full of anticipation, was back with her son.

Gandhi took a good look at the boy, and sternly told him, "Please stop eating sugar!"

Patiently, the boy's mother waited for Gandhi to say or do something else. But that was it.

"Why couldn't you tell him that two weeks ago, Mahatma?"

She asked in an exasperated voice.

"Because two weeks ago, I myself was eating sugar," Gandhi explained.

Being authentic is a precious trait.

By Zeal Okogeri

30

Be Calm

There's a Zen story of an old Chinese man who walked through a crowded marketplace with a stick over his shoulder and, on the end of the stick, a jug of soup. The crowd jostled him, and the jug fell and broke, spilling the contents.

Someone ran after the man and said, "Your jug has fallen and broken, and your soup is spilled." The informer was more excited than the old gentleman. He, with a calm typical of his ancient culture, walked straight on and said, "I know; I heard it fall!"

He simply acknowledged it, knowing the event already took place and could not be changed. There was no need to get stirred up or to create unnecessary drama. He was aware the soup could be replaced.

We can be kind to ourselves and others by not overreacting to a situation, and stirring up sudden fear, worry, panic, and despair, which are detrimental to everyone's wellbeing.

Remaining calm, especially in difficult situations, can be a profound gift of kindness to everyone involved.

By Zeal Okogeri

31

Learning to Let Go

There's a beautiful story about a wealthy couple who lived in a mansion. The couple owned eight birds they kept in a large cage in the living room. Each time they went to clean the birdcage, the birds would try to escape. One day, one of the birds successfully managed to escape. It flew toward the high ceiling and landed on a chandelier.

The couple was puzzled, for there was no way to reach the bird. As they stood wondering how to get this bird back into the cage, they noticed an ongoing communication between the birds in the cage and the free bird. The couple reasoned that the free bird was probably telling the birds in the cage to make a go for it and escape.

But after a while, the conversation intensified among the birds, and the free bird kept flying back and forth from the chandelier toward the cage. The couple then realized that the caged birds were probably urging their buddy to come back and join them. With this realization, the savvy couple opened the cage door and left the room. When they returned an hour later, the free bird had voluntarily joined the rest of his friends, again trapped inside the cage. The couple tiptoed to the birdcage and closed the door.

Often, we see the same pattern in life. When we make progress, such as overcoming an addiction, leaving a bad marriage or relationship, or quitting an unfulfilling job, the problem often lies in overcoming the hold or pulling force of those we left behind. Instead of moving forward with our newfound liberty, we allow our attachment to pull us back into a life of misery.

One of the greatest gifts of kindness that we can give ourselves and others is the willingness to let go.

The willingness and ability to let go, including letting people go, releasing them, especially when they no longer want to be with us, is a true act of love.

By Zeal Okogeri

32

The Carpool Lane

This is a story about temptation. Sometimes we know what not to do, but we do it anyway, hoping to get away with it. Well, sometimes we get away with it, and other times we don't.

It was back in the 1990s when I got an inner nudge to move to Los Angeles, California, from New Jersey. I packed my bags and was on my way to the City of Angels. I was excited and looking forward to visiting some places I had seen on TV and in the movies, like Beverly Hills, Rodeo Drive, and Hollywood, and perhaps run into some movie stars. Marina Del Rey was where I made my home. It's a beautiful part of Los Angeles, surrounded by tributaries of the Pacific Ocean, close to Venice Beach and Santa Monica, where there was lots of action. I had also enrolled in a chiropractic university in Whittier, California, about 40 minutes' drive from Marina Del Rey. This was a new beginning.

Once I got settled in, I went sightseeing in Beverly Hills and Hollywood. As I drove toward Rodeo Drive in Beverly Hills, the traffic was almost at a standstill. Gradually it started moving again. I thought there must have been an accident, but when I got to where traffic normalized, I realized there was no accident. There was something else slowing down traffic. A woman was walking her two Afghan Hound dogs. That was the first time I had ever seen an Afghan Hound. They were the most gorgeous and elegant creatures I had ever seen. Cars were slowing down to admire the dogs as they hopped elegantly like ponies with beautiful long hair parted in the middle, being blown back gently by the wind. They were like supermodels on the runway. I said to myself, "I will own a dog like these one day."

Two years later, I moved closer to school in Whittier. I found a nice single-family home, up in the hills with a great view of downtown Los Angeles. Best of all, it had a large gated backyard. "Perfect! It's time to get my Afghan Hound," I thought. I searched through the pet section of the newspapers and found advertisements for Afghans. But my goodness! I could not believe the price people were asking for an Afghan puppy, $1,500 to $3,000! As a student, I thought, "That's a price of a nice used car. Why so much money for a dog?" I later learned that Afghans are show dogs. Just to see what they looked like as puppies, I visited a breeder in Laguna Beach, Orange County. Her Afghan had given birth to five puppies. When I got there, I was in love. The puppies were all over me, climbing me like a tree, biting my legs and fingers, and falling over each other. The owner said that she normally sold them for $2,000 each, but she would let me have one for $1,200 since I was a student. I told her I'd think about it and get back to her, then left. I think she sensed the price was out of my budget.

When I returned home from school the next day, the light on my answering machine was flashing. I played the message; it was from the breeder in Laguna Beach. "I have an Afghan for you, and it's yours for free. Give me a call."

"Wow, that's fantastic!" I was excited. But then it hit me. "Why would she be giving away a $2,000 dog for free? What's wrong with it?"

I called her back right away, and without wasting any time, asked her what was wrong with the Afghan. "Well, the right front arm is bent a little, and I don't think the puppy will ever become a show dog," she said remorsefully. My mind immediately flashed back to Beverly Hills. Those dogs were perfect, no deformity whatsoever, and that was what I wanted. I was happy with her offer but disappointed that the only way I could own an Afghan was to accept one with a deformity. Nevertheless, I told her I'd come the next day to look at the puppy.

When I got to Laguna Beach and looked at the dog, I saw that it wasn't too bad. The puppy was limping but in good spirits. I reasoned that since I was becoming a chiropractic doctor at the university, it would be a great opportunity to practice on the puppy, my first non-human patient, and see if chiropractic care would be effective. So, while the breeder was instructing me on how to feed and take care of the puppy, my mind was busy contemplating a possible treatment plan to redress the deformed arm. Excited about the prospect of providing the puppy with chiropractic care, I accepted the gift with gratitude. The breeder told me to feel free to bring him back if I changed my mind, and she gave me some food to take along.

As we were driving home, the puppy looked about, making a mewing-like sound, probably wondering what had happened to his siblings. I held it closer to me as I drove so it wouldn't feel lonesome. When we got home, I fed it and began taking care of the deformed arm, using joint mobilization techniques, myofascial release, and heat therapy. The puppy was a good patient; he never complained or tried to run away during therapy.

He was a happy dog and full of energy. Perhaps too energetic. He thought my leather shoes were his toys. When I came home from school one day, I found holes in all my leather shoes, and there were torn papers and dog food everywhere. He was having a party in my absence! As I scolded him, telling him he couldn't do that again, that I needed my shoes in good condition, he was busy wagging his little tail excitedly, jumping all over me, biting my fingers, and even biting the shoes I was wearing. I gave up on the lecture.

After three months of chiropractic care, his right front leg was perfect. He was no longer limping. Six months later, my Afghan looked and behaved, just like the ones I had seen in Beverly Hills. I named him Zardin, after the legendary Afghan Hound that had been presented to the royal family of England in 1907. We became inseparable companions. Soon we were going for long walks and runs, and he was racing around open grounds with other dogs. Incidentally, the Afghan Hound breed is originally from Afghanistan. They are hunting dogs and very fast. Zardin always left other dogs panting whenever they tried keeping up with him.

I had a two-seater sports car in those days, and Zardin always sat next to me, on the passenger seat. Because of his beautiful long hair that blew about in the wind as we drove around, people easily mistook him for a woman when they saw him from the back. That was until they saw his long nose on a side view. I was often asked by friends, "Who was the lady I saw you driving around with?" I'd explain it was my dog, Zardin, and we'd have a good laugh.

One day I was in my former neighborhood, Marina Del Rey, with Zardin, returning to my school in Whittier. I had an exam that afternoon and wanted to make it back to school on time. However, there was bumper-to-bumper traffic on Freeway 101, by the Los Angeles Airport. The traffic was so congested; it took almost an hour to cover one mile. I was getting frustrated, knowing I was about to miss my exam. When I looked over at the two carpool lanes, I saw they were practically empty, cars were zooming by at high speed. That's when temptation set in. I took another look at my dog with his lovely long hair, "Mmm, everybody mistakes you for a woman, don't they?" Next thing I knew, I was cruising down the carpool lane with Zardin. We hadn't gone more than a mile when I looked in my rear-view mirror and noticed a police car approaching in the left carpool lane. I turned to Zardin. "I think we are in big trouble." He looked at me with his head tilted to one side, wondering what I was talking about.

As the police car passed, I tried my best not to make eye contact with the officer. But from my peripheral vision, I saw that the officer casually peeked into my car. Not believing what he saw, he quickly took another look and shook his head in dismay.

"PULL OVER! PULL OVER!" blasted through the loudspeakers of his vehicle. The officer turned on every flashing light on the vehicle, along with sirens. He halted traffic in all six lanes of the freeway and, with his car bumper, literally pushed my car to the far-right side of the highway. At that point, I forgot all about my exam. There was a much bigger problem at hand.

Looking through my rear-view mirror, I saw the officer

getting out of his vehicle. With one hand placed on top of his firearm, he approached my vehicle and motioned me to roll down my window. My dog started barking at the sight of the officer: woof, woof, woof.

"Calm your dog down!" demanded the police officer. I pleaded with my dog. "Zardin, please calm down, this is a law enforcement officer." I hoped he would understand. Reluctantly, he stopped barking, sat down, and continued growling, upset that somebody in uniform was disturbing his best friend.

"Sir, what are you doing?" asked the officer bewildered.

"What do you mean?" I replied, quite innocently.

Turning red in the face, he said, "Sir, you were driving in the carpool lane! The carpool lane is for two or more passengers."

"Yes, I know, there's my dog and me, two passengers!"

At this point, the officer's face was so red I thought he was going to explode. Trying his best to hold back expletives, he implored, rapidly raising his voice as he went on, "Sir, the carpool lane is for two people! Two people! It's not for one man and a bird. It's not for one man and a cat. And it's not for one man and a dog! It's for two people, two people!"

"I'm sorry, officer! I'm sorry!" I started apologizing, realizing I had caused much irritation to a truly dedicated policeman.

Hearing my accent, he asked in a calmer, more caring tone, "Sir, where are you from?"

As soon as I said, 'West Africa,' he raised his arms in the air and cried out, "It figures!"

"Let me explain something to you, Sir," he leaned toward me and continued, now speaking to me slowly, as if I couldn't understand English, and in a hushed tone, as if confiding a secret: "I really don't care what you guys do in your carpool lanes in Africa. I really don't care. I don't care if you have one man and a giraffe, one man and a goat, or one man and a chicken. I don't care! But here in Los Angeles, it's two people! Two people! Do you understand, Sir?"

The officer was clearly upset. Each time he said, "Two people!" he would show me two fingers, to make sure there was no misunderstanding.

"I completely understand, officer," I humbly reassured him.

"How long have you lived in Los Angeles?" he queried.

"Three months, officer."

"Well, you've been here long enough to know better, so I'm going to give you a ticket. But I'm giving you a break this time. Normally the fine is more than $300, but I'm going to give you a ticket for $168 as a warning."

"Thank you, officer!" I said, a bit relieved. Observing my demeanor, my dog sensed the problem was resolved. Reenergized, he stood on the passenger seat and started barking again: woof, woof, woof. But this time, the bark was much softer, as if he didn't mean it. It was unclear to me whether the dog was thanking the officer on my behalf for being kind, or whether he was still trying to chase away the officer. In any case, we accepted the ticket and were on our way.

When I got to school and explained to my classmates why I had missed the exam, they just couldn't stop laughing, oblivious to the big fine I had to pay. They said it was the most hilarious story they've heard in a long time.

But I learned my lesson. Ever since that fateful day, before

I enter a carpool lane, I always make sure my passengers are humans. I have no intentions of ever driving alone in the carpool lane with a dog, a bird, a cat, or a member of the wildlife—not even in carpool lanes in Africa.

Temptations come in different forms, and if not resisted, can be very costly.

The experience was also an excellent lesson on how we create karma for ourselves.

By Zeal Okogeri

Chapter Five

FOLLOW YOUR HEART

Follow your heart. Life is too short to be sidetracked by the things everyone else wants you to do.

— Anonymous

33

Follow Your Heart

A few years ago, I facilitated a workshop at the San Francisco Convention Center. On my way back to San Diego, I made a new friend, Paul, on the plane. He told me a story that touched me deeply.

As soon as the plane took off, Paul started a conversation with me. He was a nurse in the cardiology department of a major hospital in San Jose, California, and was traveling to San Diego with his wife and daughter for a vacation. He shared touching experiences from his work that emphasized how people should not take life for granted. For example, he had seen many young executives come into the hospital complaining of simple problems like neck pain and then being diagnosed with an aneurysm. Before long, some of these patients died of heart trouble. He said he'd learned that people should not waste their lives waiting for conditions to be perfect before embarking on their purpose.

As Paul and I continued to talk, he told me more about his life. Immediately after serving in the Vietnam War in the 1960s, Paul, now in his 50s, had enrolled in college. Ever since he had been a little boy, he had dreamt of traveling the world, but conditions were never right. There was always the financial concern. Then, as part of his nursing training, he went on a class trip to visit several cancer clinics in Mexico. There he had an opportunity to interview dying cancer patients.

The question Paul posed to the patients was, "Now that you have lived your life up to this point and are dying of cancer, what advice would you give those who are healthy and living?"

Although the patients' words differed, their message was all the same. "Find whatever your passion is and go for it now, and don't worry about money. If there is anything, you have always wanted to do, if there is anything important to you that you have been putting off, go and do it. Don't waste any more time. If you wait until conditions are just right, you may not have your health by then." Some of these patients deeply regretted not having the courage to live their dreams, not having the courage to express their true feelings, not being true to their needs, compromising the richness of their lives by becoming workaholics, and not sharing enough time with family and friends, among other things.

Moved by the encounter, Paul returned from the field trip, liquidated half of his savings account, and set out to travel the world. On a tight budget, he stayed with families he met along the way and in youth hostels. "I had the best time of my life," he said to me.

Back in school the following semester, Paul invited his chemistry professor, with whom he had developed a special friendship, to view a slide show of his travels. The professor was impressed; "Where the hell did you get an idea like this?" Paul told his professor about his life-changing field trip to the cancer clinics in Mexico. The two maintained their close friendship until Paul graduated.

Five years later, Paul ran into his old friend, the college chemistry professor. By this time, his professor had resigned his position at the university, gotten a divorce, sold his house, taken a trip around the world, and met and fallen in love with a real princess from South America. The man was so happy he could hardly contain himself. Paul and his former professor had a wonderful time catching up with each other's lives and reflecting on their life journeys.

Twenty years later, Paul was working in the hospital and thought he heard his name being called. Someone was struggling to get his attention. He heard a long, drawn-out "P-a-u-l . . . P-a- u-l . . . P-a-u-l." He started walking toward the voice and saw an old, gray-haired man in a wheelchair with tubes protruding from his abdomen. He had a difficult time recognizing the man. The old man struggled as he said, "P-a-u-l, I just want to thank you for inspiring me to travel. If it weren't for you, I would never have seen the world." By the side of this frail, gray-haired man was a beautiful lady 20 years his junior, his South American princess bride.

As the plane began its descent toward San Diego, Paul mused, "This thing called life is so precious, and it goes so fast." He turned and said to me, "You really can't afford to put off your dreams any longer."

By Zeal Okogeri

34

Love All

When I traveled to India a few years ago, I had four specific places I wanted to visit. The Lotus Temple, the spiritual hub of the Bahá'í faith, in New Delhi; the Golden Temple, the spiritual center of the Sikhism religion, in Amritsar, Punjab; the Radha Soami Satsang headquarters in Beas; and the Ruhani Satsang in New Delhi. Visiting each of these spiritual centers was transformative. At Ruhani Satsang, I bought a small book on the teaching of the Light and Sound Current and a blue pen. On the side of the pen was inscribed in bold gold letters, LUV ALL. I felt it said everything that needed to be said.

Two years after returning to the States, I experienced a health concern and visited a hospital in Honolulu, Hawaii. After going through emergency care, I was admitted to the hospital. As I laid in bed wondering about my fate, a gracious middle-aged physician walked in. I could tell from her facial features that she's probably from India. Smiling, she asked where I'm originally from, and I told her that I was born in a village in southeastern Nigeria. Then I asked her if she was from India.

"Yes," she said joyfully.

I indicated that I visited India for the first time two years ago. She was delighted to hear that and inquired about which part of India I had visited. When I mentioned that I was at the Rhada Soami Satsang headquarters in Beas, Punjab, she was overcome with emotion. "All my family members belong to Rhada Soami, and when I was a young girl, I was also a devoted member and felt connected to the teachings. But after I came to America, got into medical school and a career, life got very busy, and somehow, I drifted away from it." She seemed remorseful like she had lost something very precious. "I need to get back to practicing again," she affirmed. Our conversation got so deep so fast and had us so connected and transported to a distant land that she forgot, momentarily, that she had come into the room to see a patient. About 10 minutes later, she regained her awareness, snapped back from the journey which the Divine had orchestrated for us, and with a somewhat embarrassed smile said, "I'm so sorry, but what brought you to the hospital?" Being aware of how Spirit often works, I simply smiled and provided her with my medical history.

The next morning, right after the lab technician left my room, another female doctor walked in wearing a hijab, a headscarf worn by Muslim women. Like the Rhada Soami doctor of the day before, the Muslim doctor was caring, understanding, and knowledgeable. After she examined me and offered insight into my health, she wished me well and encouraged me to contact her by phone if I developed new symptoms.

When she left my room to attend to other patients, I began reflecting on my interaction with the two doctors, the many nurses, and the other specialists who came to my room to provide services. It's interesting how the hospital evokes deep reflections; perhaps it's because the threat to life allows one to contemplate on what's important in life. You find that you think less about the material aspects of life and more about the people in your life and the quality of your relationship with them. Life begins to look more and more like it's all about your relationship with people. And as you reflect, you begin to gain clarity on those you love and those who love you. Often it is your sincere desire to see and be with those you love that expedites your recovery.

Anyway, I reflected on how the hospital personnel consisted of people of all backgrounds—different cultures, nationalities, ethnicities, and religions.

It saddened me to observe that when we are comfortable, and relatively in good health, we have the luxury of judging and condemning people based on their culture, skin color, religion, etc. We become ethnocentric and intolerant; we label other's religions as cults, perhaps because they don't follow the doctrine of our faith. We try to maintain our distance from 'those people' whom we see as anti-God. But when life kicks our butt, when we get sick and desperate for help, suddenly, as if struck by lightning, we let go of our prejudices. Skin color, ethnicity, and religious affiliation don't matter anymore. We don't refuse help from a Rhada Soami doctor or a Muslim doctor wearing a hijab and demand doctors of our faith. No, we are so happy that a doctor, any doctor (whether he or she belongs to a 'cult'), has come to take care of us. The same goes for the nurses and the host of other healthcare practitioners who come to our aid; after all, no one wears a badge displaying their religious or spiritual affiliation.

"Why do we behave this way?" I kept wondering. When we

are desperate and need help, anyone is acceptable, but when life is good, we judge and practice racism. When we are old, injured, or disabled, anyone and everyone are welcome to be our caretaker, including the same people we rejected not so long ago. Why?

My hospital stays allowed me to realize how we deliberately or through our ignorance, cut ourselves off from love. We push people away, potential angels in disguise because their physical characteristics, background, or religion don't meet our expectations. We see the physical body. Unfortunately, we don't know who is wearing the physical body. If we did, I believe we would be humbled. I'm reminded of a Hindu proverb, "If God needed a perfect place to hide, It would hide inside a human being because no one will ever look there." The physical body is the greatest disguise, for it hides the magnificence of the spirit or soul wearing it. Because of this, you never really know who you are dealing with.

As I rested in my hospital bed contemplating all this, part of me was amused, suggesting that I was an idealist; after all, this is earth, an imperfect place, a playground for embodied spirits. But a deeper part of me gently interjected and reassured me that we can transcend the little self, the slippery illusions of the ego, and other passions of the mind that undermine harmony. It all depends on how much we are willing to love. Then I was reminded of the golden inscription on the blue pen I bought two years earlier at the Ruhani Satsang in New Delhi, LUV ALL.

By Zeal Okogeri

35

The Last Customer

I owned a small neighborhood grocery store in a community where everyone knew most everyone. Over the years, I got to know my loyal customers who stopped by each day to pick up fresh fruits and vegetables. One morning while driving to work, I was waiting at a stoplight across the street from my store at a busy intersection. Out of the corner of my eye, I saw a homeless woman dressed in a long, colorful skirt and a matching headwrap. She stood out and captured my attention. I had driven through this town on this busy main street hundreds of times before but had never seen this lady in my life. "Who is this woman, and where did she come from?" I thought to myself as I felt a sense of sadness wash over me. Immediately, my heart went out to her; so did my curiosity. I have seen a few homeless people living in the neighborhood, but never a woman. I became concerned for her safety because I knew the area was not always the safest at night. I never kept my store open past 7 p.m. because the neighborhood drew in a different crowd at night.

On my way home that evening, there she was, sleeping on a blanket with only a few of her belongings surrounding her makeshift bed on a sidewalk. She slept in the same spot where I had seen her earlier that morning, next to an old green building with bright fluorescent lights hanging from the corrugated roof awning. I would have thought that anyone sleeping under those bright lights would not get much sleep, but then I realized she might have picked this spot for her safety since it was well-lit and highly visible to those driving by. I felt an inner nudge telling me to help her, and I said to myself that tomorrow I would give her some food or money.

The next morning on my way to work, I looked for her along the main street but did not see her. That evening on my way home after a long day of work, I looked over and saw that she was already sleeping. I told myself, "I'll try tomorrow once again." The next morning when I drove to work, she was already gone.

Days became weeks, and I always seemed to miss her. Some days I would see her through my window blinds, but I was too busy with customers and day-to-day operations. One afternoon, I decided to close the shop for a few minutes to pick up lunch at a nearby eatery. From a far distance, I saw her sitting on the opposite side of the street a couple of blocks away from her usual spot. "Finally!" I said to myself. This was my opportunity to help. I did not have any cash on me, so I headed back to my store to get some funds. When I opened my cash register, I took the only $20 bill inside the drawer. I folded the bill in half, placed it in an envelope, and sealed it. Across the front, I wrote, "God Bless You." As I walked to where she was sitting, I noticed she was reading a book. As I took a closer look, I came to realize it was not just any book; she was reading the Holy Bible.

I politely said, "Hello," as she slowly gazed up at me. Her face remained expressionless, but her eyes were deep and intense as if they told a story. I felt an instant connection to her when she looked into my eyes. I sensed she was a strong-willed woman who has been through many adversities in this life. Something about her presence was powerful. I felt in my spirit that she was a woman with unshakable faith—a woman of God. "This is for you," I said as I handed her the envelope. She reached out and took the enveloped from my hand and nodded in acknowledgment. I turned around and headed back to work.

As I began closing the store for the evening, I turned off the open sign. When I proceeded to lock the front entrance door, I heard the doorbell chime. Before I could say, "I'm sorry, we are closed," to my surprise, it was the mysterious woman I had seen earlier that day. She was standing in front of me. I fumbled for words and greeted her: "Good evening, ma'am."

She nodded and proceeded to pick up a shopping basket. From behind the counter, I could not help but watch as she took her time picking items from the aisles and carefully studying the price of each item. I did not mind staying open for her. My heart raced, as I could not believe this woman I had been seeking out was now in my store. She could have shopped at the other stores around the neighborhood, but she picked my store. As she walked to the counter to pay for the items, I thought about not charging her and to bless her once again, but in my spirit, something told me, "Allow her to bless you this time." As I rang up her items on the cash register and gave her the total, she pulled out a coin purse from her plastic bag filled with clothes and her few other possessions. She placed her coin purse on the counter and slowly unzipped it. I wanted to strike up a conversation with her or to see if she remembered me from earlier that day, but she remained quiet. In her coin purse, I could see a handful of coins and a neatly folded bill. She slowly unwrapped the bill – a $20 bill. It was the only bill she had in her coin purse.

I was happy and sad at the same time. I was glad that she had money to buy dinner that evening. But saddened because she may not have been able to buy dinner had I again found myself too busy with work or found an excuse to hold off for another day. Still, I know God's timing is always perfect, and He provides for the needs of those who have faith in Him. I know this for myself because I have been through obstacles in my life that I never thought I could overcome, but He has always sent people in my direction to encourage me. At times, I felt alone. I felt as if my spirit was broken, but then I would read my Bible, and God would give me peace. This woman exuded the same peace and confidence despite being homeless because of her faith in God. Perhaps, that's why I felt such a connection with her. As the woman left my store, I sat back in my chair for a few moments to reflect on everything that had just happened. I had witnessed with my very own eyes how blessing others will find its way back to you, and I was in awe of God's goodness. Receiving the $20 bill back from the person I gave it to was worth more to me than its face value. My spirit was uplifted, and my faith renewed. To me, this encounter was priceless. When we share and show love and kindness to others, God is already orchestrating a plan to bless us even more.

In the following days and weeks, I looked for her, but I never again saw this mysterious woman dressed in a long, colorful skirt and a matching headwrap. I could not help but wonder if I had been visited by an angel.

"Let brotherly love always continue. Do not neglect to show kindness to strangers; for, in this way, some without knowing it, have had angels as their guest." Hebrew 13:1-2.

By Jennifer Miguel

36

Lover of All Life

There was a village known for its great warriors. Young men aspired to become great hunters and to set new hunting records. For a man, to gain a reputation for courage by killing huge, ferocious animals was a source of great honor and prestige. The village warriors showed their strength and social standing by wearing animal artifacts and decorating their homes with animal skeletons, skins, horns, and tusks.

There was a man in this village who, although a natural-born warrior, refused to hunt. He preferred to farm. The villagers ridiculed him for being different and called him obnoxious names, but he wasn't bothered by the name-calling. He refused to hunt because he loved animals. He considered them his own family and the thought of killing them was unimaginable. He always said that when he retired, he would build a hut in the wilderness and live with his extended family—the animals.

As time went on, he became a quite successful farmer and gained a reputation for great harvests. When retirement came, he kept his promise and announced that he was ready to build his hut in the wilderness. Many laughed at him for having such a ridiculous ambition. Following his send-off ceremony, which was not well attended, a few members of his village escorted him into the wilderness and left him there.

He constructed a small hut and began his long stay in the wilderness. A week went by and he began to feel lonely. He was all by himself. He began to wonder if he had made a terrible mistake by leaving behind his village, family, relatives, and friends.

One day, after having lunch, he went outside and threw the leftovers in front of his hut. Not knowing what else to do, he plucked a blade of grass and chewed on its fresh sweetness. Overwhelmed by loneliness, he wandered into the hut and sat down, gazing alternately between the floor and the roof, wondering about his destiny.

Just then, he noticed a movement in his peripheral vision. Three lions were feeding on the leftovers he had thrown out. He could not believe his eyes! His attitude changed and he sprang back to life. 'My family finally came to say hello,' he thought happily to himself. After the lions finished eating and walked away, another group of animals, including antelopes and giraffes, came and ate some leaves in the area. Then the birds flew in to pick on whatever they could find on the ground.

For the first time in his life, the old man felt he had done something truly significant. Overjoyed, he devoted his life to feeding the animals. He got in the habit of preparing breakfast, lunch, and dinner and taking it out for the animals on a daily basis. The animals got to know and trust him to the point that they ate out of his hands. He, too, trusted the animals; he never closed the door to his hut, even at night. They were truly a family. He served the animals for nearly 20 years. By this time, he had grown very old and had to use a walking cane. His old age became a major concern to him because he had no successor.

One day, as luck would have it, two hunters were passing by and noticed a hut in the depths of the jungle. It dawned on them that they had discovered the home of the notorious strange man who loved animals. "Let's pay him a visit," they said to each other. The old man was elated to see human beings for the first time in 20 years. A gracious host, he brought out for his visitors a large basket of fruits he had grown. As they exchanged pleasantries, the old man confided in them his dilemma and asked the two men to find out if anyone would be interested in taking over his work in the wilderness.

When the old man's predicament was announced in the village, three young men immediately volunteered out of great respect. However, as it was customary for the elders to engage in long periods of reflection before eventually reaching a decision, the volunteers were asked to wait for seven days while the elders conferred with the oracle. Seven days later, all was well, and the volunteers were on their way to relieve the old man.

It was an emotional goodbye for a man who had served his animal family for nearly 20 years. As he was escorted away from the jungle, he kept turning around and waving to the vast forest, apologizing that age would not allow him to continue doing what he loved more than anything else on earth. Tears poured down his cheeks as he remembered the great times he had shared with the animals, knowing he would never see them again. When he arrived at the village with his entourage, he was recognized for his great love and compassion for the animals and given a hero's welcome. Everyone was abuzz with celebration as the old man toured his village, accompanied by colorful masquerade and dancers. Food and wine were in abundance. No one in the history of the village had ever demonstrated such love.

The three volunteers, meanwhile, carried out the job in the wilderness to the best of their ability. Upon arising one morning, they encountered a most startling sight. Animals were everywhere, thousands of them! This was most unusual, for the animals usually came in twos or threes to feed, never in the thousands. As if that was not enough, there were so many birds hovering in the air that it was impossible to see the beautiful blue sky. It was an unprecedented sight! They were quietly parading around the hut where the old man had lived. Even animals that were natural enemies got along surprisingly well on this incredible day.

The three volunteers were stunned. They wondered if they had done something terribly wrong. The parade continued for almost an hour, after which the animals and birds peacefully dispersed into the vast wilderness.

As the volunteers pondered the unprecedented event, they saw a messenger from the village approaching. Before they had a chance to share with the messenger what had just taken place in the forest, the messenger said, "I'm sorry, but I am bringing bad news. The old man passed away early this morning."

Nature responded by staging a parade around the hut to honor and pay its final respects to a lover of all life.

Nature never forgets your actions, the folklore affirms. It records and remembers everything you do, and in the end honors you accordingly.

By Zeal Okogeri

Chapter Six

COUNT YOUR
BLESSINGS

There is a blessing hidden in every trial in life,
but you have to be willing to open
your heart to see them.

—Anonymous

37

Think Again Before Beating Yourself Up

When I was in my 20s, I founded a computer export company and was exporting computer accessories to Saudi Arabia, Greece, and Nigeria. Later, I established a fully staffed subsidiary of my company in Victoria Island, Lagos, Nigeria. I traveled a lot during those days. I often wondered what day it was as I journeyed from one country to the other. I visited Greece and Nigeria often because my younger brother was studying in Athens at the time, and I would pass through Athens on my way to visit my company in Lagos. During one such trip, I was on my way back to the United States from Nigeria, with a stopover in Athens. I checked into the Sheraton Hotel in Ikeja, Lagos. The next morning, I was scheduled to take a flight with Egypt Air to Athens. Usually, I'm meticulous when it comes to organizing my flights and making sure I get to the airport on time because I know the inconvenience that goes with missing international flights. Thus, I never miss an international flight.

The night before my departure, I packed my luggage and was ready. All I had to do the next morning was take a shower, get dressed, and check out of my hotel. Since my flight was scheduled to depart at 10 a.m., I called the lobby and scheduled a wakeup call for 6 a.m. As a contingency, I set my travel alarm clock for 6 a.m. I reasoned that if I woke up at 6 a.m. and left the hotel by 7 a.m., I'd have plenty of time to get to the airport, check-in, and have breakfast before my departure.

To my astonishment, I woke up the next morning at 9:45 a.m. My flight would be in the air in 15 minutes. With traffic, it could take from half an hour to an hour to get to the airport. I could not believe it. In utter disbelief, I called the lobby to find out the correct time because my clock couldn't possibly be accurate. They confirmed it was almost 10 a.m. I angrily inquired why they hadn't called me as scheduled. They apologized, saying they'd been calling my room every half hour since 6 a.m. I was well-known to the hotel staff because I stayed at their hotel regularly. My alarm clock indicated it had performed as well.

I was obviously in such a deep state of sleep that I hadn't heard any of it. This had never happened in all my years of traveling. With no one else to blame, I started beating myself up. I called myself every unflattering name I could think of. "What's wrong with you? Why do you need 12 hours of sleep, for goodness' sakes?" I was so upset because of all the inconveniences I was about to face. I had to notify my brother in Athens that I was no longer arriving as planned. I had to book a hotel room for an additional night, assuming I could get a flight for the next day. Besides, I knew I would likely pay the airline penalty fees for changing my departure date. I hadn't planned to spend more money. You can imagine how frustrated and upset I was. Fortunately, I was able to reschedule my flight for the next day, but the penalty fee was high.

Not knowing what to do for the day, I decided to hire a car

with a driver, as is often done in Lagos, and went sightseeing. I came back in the evening. Upon entering my hotel room, I turned on the television. There was breaking news. The flight I had missed that morning had crash-landed in Cairo! "What?" My mouth flew wide open. My eyes were glued to the TV, and my legs went limp as I sat on my bed in disbelief. Although no one was killed, I felt sad for the onboard passengers and those who were wounded. At the same time, I was filled with profound gratitude that the Divine had spared me that horrible experience. I couldn't thank God enough. Here I was beating myself up, not knowing that the Divine had my back and caused me to oversleep.

That experience taught me a very important life lesson. As humans, we often react negatively and sometimes violently when things don't go our way or when we work so hard to make a relationship work or to fulfill our dream, and it does not materialize. But now, I share the lesson I've learned with others: No matter how terrible an experience might be, whether it is a job loss, a missed flight, a most cherished relationship that ended abruptly, or any other of life's many unforeseen calamities or disappointments, before you start beating yourself up and regretting, think again! Maybe, just maybe, it was for your own good!

With Blessings.

By Zeal Okogeri

38

Crossing
into U.S. Airspace

Having flown as a flight attendant for PAN AM and Delta for 45 years before retiring a few years ago, I, like many other veteran flight attendants, have so many stories to tell that I could write volumes. What I miss about flying are the many interesting people and the conversations I've had over the years. Especially with the wonderful military personnel we had on board the CRAF (Civil Reserve Air Fleet) flights on which we either took soldiers to the Middle East or brought them home. It was always far better to bring them home; I can assure you.

The very first CRAF flight I flew was a 747 from Saudi Arabia to JFK, where we picked up members of the 82nd Airborne, from the Gulf War, all men, with their huge unloaded and well-polished AK47 assault rifles by their seats. We, flight attendants, used all kinds of things to decorate the interior of the plane to make it as festive as possible for the soldiers. The plane captain had also gone out of his way to arrange to bring onboard 25 cases of Budweiser, ready to give each military man a celebratory beer, compliments of the captain! Before taking off, the captain enthusiastically introduced himself to the military commander, letting him know about the cases of beer so that we could bring them up to the galleys. Sadly, the commander declined the offer. He wanted his men sober. The captain was disappointed, but it's the thought that counts.

Once we were in the air, and after several hours of flying, several of the servicemen asked if we could ask the captain to "PLEASE let us know when we have crossed over to the U.S. air space!" We called the captain several times and reminded him to tell the military men when we were in U.S. air space. In the meantime, a couple of us flight attendants were in the big back galley talking to about 20 of the guys.

All of a sudden, the captain's voice came over the intercom and announced, "Gentlemen, we have just crossed into U.S. airspace." When the announcement came, you could hear a pin drop in the cabin, as there was momentarily complete silence. Then many of the military passengers were wiping tears from their faces, while others were struggling to hold back tears. We, flight attendants, were in tears too. Then there were hugs all around from the men who were in the galley with us and others who stood from the seats! Applause burst out next. It was very moving because the soldiers had fought so hard and for a long time under such awful conditions that many of them never thought they'd see home again.

Unbeknownst to me, I had been talking to a captain who asked just then if I would consider trading my uniform wings for his red 82nd Airborne beret and parachute wings. "ABSOLUTELY!" He could have had anything! I took my PAN AM wings off my uniform while he went to get his beret and wings.

It was a privilege each time to bring these men and women home, and it always felt better bringing them home than taking them to war. We felt so much joy along with soldiers to touch down on U.S. soil. GOD BLESS AMERICA AND ALL WHO HAVE AND CONTINUE TO SERVE IT.

The day I retired from my 45-year flying career, I joined the USO (United Service Organizations), so I could continue serving our military at the Atlanta airport one day a month. It is the least the volunteers and I can do for these wonderful men and women who pass through the airport regularly.

By Beverly MacKay

39

Compassion for the Homeless

My husband of 46 years has always been a man who selflessly helps others. He inherited this trait from his parents, who were also kind and giving and set an example throughout his childhood of how easy it is to find a need and fill it. I have witnessed his generous acts of kindness on many occasions. It always fosters warm emotions in my heart and uplifted the recipients of his kindness.

My husband has a soft spot in his heart for the homeless. He works in Seattle and drives all day through the downtown area, where countless destitute folks are standing in the cold rain on the corners, holding signs asking for help. We have both had unfortunate experiences in which we helped someone, only to realize later that it was a scam. My husband has found a way around this. He buys large bags of new thick socks at Costco and keeps them under the seat in his van. Instead of giving money to the sign carriers, he hands them a pair of socks. Can you imagine what clean, soft socks would mean to someone homeless? To have warm, fresh, dirt-free foot protection is a simple gift but meaningful in unknown ways to the recipient. Most of the time, he is greeted with a "Thanks, man" or a "God bless" accompanied by a warm smile. The heart-to-heart connection is deeply moving to both the giver and the receiver.

Another way he helps the homeless is to pick someone up off the street and take them into a restaurant, sit with them, and buy them lunch or dinner. He engages the person in conversation and lets them know they are worthy. My husband and his guest quite often receive wary or angry stares from other patrons because the homeless person is usually not dressed 'appropriately,' and most likely is a bit grimy for dining. My accommodating husband proudly escorts his new friend to a booth where he tells his friend to order anything off the menu. The time together usually consists of conversations which often bring to light the person's story, or merely eating in silence, if this is what the person wants. The much-needed full belly and human validation are warm reminders of our connection to every soul on earth, no matter what our paths in life.

A few years ago, my husband decided he wanted a change from our Thanksgiving tradition and asked if I would mind serving the homeless with him at a shelter in Seattle. I felt this would be a welcome break from the large family gatherings and traditional gluttony, so I heartily agreed. When we got to the shelter, there was an overabundance of helpers, so we were feeling a bit misplaced. My husband saw large boxes of oranges and apples and asked the servers if we could take them to the streets and hand them out to those who had declined the shelter meal. They agreed, and we headed out to Pioneer Square in the pouring rain to give our small offerings to the destitute souls in our city. We met drug addicts, alcoholics, and mentally ill and depressed folks. I was hesitant to approach them but followed my husband's lead and found these humans to be approachable, likable, and gracious. This experience was a gift to me from my husband, and I cherish the unexpected connections still.

As a Vietnam war veteran and a retired Coast Guard man, my husband also has a warm spot in his heart for the hardships of military personnel and their families. We were in a restaurant once when a clean-cut young man in army uniform came in with his wife, two small children, and parents. Because of the joy and affection the family displayed, it was apparent that the soldier had just returned from overseas and might even be deploying again soon. We watched them basking in the simple ritual of dining together and wondered what their story was. When the waitress came with our check, my husband said he wanted to pay anonymously for the entire family's meal. We sat and watched as the waitress told the man his bill was taken care of. A look of surprise and astonishment flickered across his face, and then his eyes slowly scanned the room until he recognized a kindred soul in my husband.

As the family got up to leave, the soldier came over to our table and saluted my husband, who respectfully acknowledged the salute and offered one back. For me, this was goosebumps (God bump) moment, and it still brings tears to my eyes when I relate it. It is easy to give your heart to others. It doesn't take great effort or even require that you reveal that you have done so. If you look around, you will see many opportunities to give a compliment or just smile at a stranger. Our world is in desperate need of loving-kindness and heart-to-heart human connection. I learn this every day from my husband, and I'm blessed to have him as a shining example of what it means to be human.

By Margie Pasero

40

A Mysterious Stranger at Tiananmen Square

I just purchased my train ticket and was excited to travel to Lhasa, Tibet, from Beijing, China. This will be my first time in Tibet and the longest train journey I've ever taken, 48 hours one way! Since it was 3 p.m. and my train didn't leave until 8 p.m., I had some time for sightseeing at Tiananmen Square, Beijing.

After two hours of sightseeing, at about 5 p.m., I thought I should get going. I expected to get to my hotel by 5:30 p.m. and proceeding to the train station by 6 p.m. What I never anticipated was that rush hour started at 5 p.m. and getting a taxi would be nearly impossible. It was getting late, and still no cab. Worried that I'll miss my train to Tibet, I walked to a nearby bus station and gave my hotel business card to a bus driver. Speaking in broken Chinese, I inquired which bus was going near my hotel. She wrote number 59 on a piece of paper and handed to me and provided directions in Chinese. Fortunately, she used a lot of hand gestures because I didn't understand one thing she said. With a vague idea of where to find bus stop 59, I walked on. When I got to the general area, the street was blocked. Frustrated, I said out loud, "What do I do now?"

Immediately, I felt a tap on my left shoulder. I turned and saw a serious-looking Chinese boy of about ten years old. He was wearing a backpack and spoke rapidly in English, "Are you looking for bus number 49?"

"No, number 59," I responded, rather surprised.

"Follow me!" he commanded and sped away. He walked so fast; I practically jogged to keep up with him. He led me around the rush hour traffic congestion, marching like a soldier. On one occasion, he confidently raised his right arm, halting traffic and leading me across a three-lane street. Crazy Beijing drivers obeyed him! It was unbelievable. He led me to a bus stop where people were standing in a queue and ordered me to stand behind a man, one of the passengers waiting for bus number 59.

As soon as he completed the task, he waved goodbye. He didn't say a word, just turned around and walked away. I ran after him, calling on him to wait, and offering him money for his kindness. He was offended. He looked at me with such disgust, as if to say, "What the hell are you doing? You think I need to get paid for helping you?" He adamantly rejected the money and marched on to his next destination.

Later I wondered where the stranger came from and how he could have known that I was looking for a bus, let alone mentioning bus number 49. I had been walking for a while, perhaps 15 minutes. To this day, I can't figure out where this Chinese boy came from and how he knew I was looking for a bus. My gratitude remains boundless for the relentless generosities of Spirit.

This experience was a beautiful reminder that we are never alone in this journey called life. We are always under spiritual surveillance. The more we trust in this unwavering guidance and protection of Spirit, the more we experience the miracles of life.

By Zeal Okogeri

41

Chicken or Eagle?

There's a beautiful story about a farmer who lived in a remote village. One day he decided to climb the cliffs that brooded above the valley to see what lay beyond.

He climbed all day until he reached a ledge just below the top of the cliff; there, to his amazement, was a nest with an egg in it.

He thought the nest must have fallen from a nearby tree. From the shape and size, he knew it was an eagle's egg that may have been abandoned by the mother. With compassion, he carefully took the egg and stowed it in his backpack; then, seeing that the sun was low in the sky, he realized it was too late in the day to make it to the top and slowly began his way down the cliff to his farm.

When he got home, he put the egg in with other eggs that one of his chickens was sitting on. Although the egg was bigger than all the other eggs, the mother hen proudly sat on it. Sure enough, some weeks later, from the eggs emerged fine, healthy chicks and one eaglet.

As the eagle grew up with its brother and sister chicks, it learned to do all the things chickens do: it clucked and cackled, scratching in the dirt for grits and worms, flapping its wings furiously, flying just a few feet in the air before crashing down to earth in a pile of dust and feathers.

It believed resolutely and absolutely that it was a chicken. One day he was with his fellow chickens picking seeds off the ground when a shadow covered the sky above him. He lifted his gaze and was mesmerized by the sight of a beautiful eagle cruising the sky. Unlike other chicken that he saw trying to fly, this eagle didn't seem to be making much effort. With his wings spread wide, he was flying smoothly and changing his direction with the slightest gesture. "Wow. Look at that!" yelled the young eagle to his friends. "What is that?" he asked. "That's an eagle," replied a chicken. "He's the king of the sky.

The young eagle was very impressed as it stared at the magnificent bird disappearing in the horizon as if gliding on an invisible path that only he could see. "How wonderful it must be to fly like an eagle!" exclaimed the young eagle.

"Yes, it must be nice, but forget it because you are a chicken!" replied mother hen.

With that, the young eagle continued to live its life as a chicken but could never get the memory of the magnificent eagle out of his mind.

One day, the farmer came by the barn to see how the young eagle was doing. He felt sad and heartbroken to see the young eagle running with other chickens and hiding in the barnyard because an eagle had surged to the ground.

The old man asked the young eagle, "What are you doing?"

"We're hiding from the eagle before it attacks us."

"Hiding? Why?"

"You're the same as the one you're hiding from!"

"What do you mean?" replied the young one.

"You are an eagle! Look at your feet; look at your feathers.

Do you look like a chicken?"

"I am a chicken. These are my brothers and sisters. I grew up with them."

"No, you're not. You're an eagle. You belong in the sky, not on the ground."

"No, I am not. I am one of them. All I know is to do as they do and to eat what they eat. I can't even fly."

With that, the farmer sat the young eagle down and told him the story of how it had come to live with chickens. "I was only trying to save your life; that's why I brought you here," explained the farmer. "Now it's time for you to realize who you are. Get ready; we are leaving early tomorrow morning. I will show you where I found you."

The next day, the farmer began climbing the cliff with the young eagle standing on his right shoulder. When they got to the very spot where the farmer found the egg, he said to the eagle, "Your training begins today, and we'll stay here until your wings are strong enough to set you free."

The young eagle was doubtful and scared. A part of him was sad about his brothers and sisters—the chickens at the barn—that he was leaving behind. They were all he knew since birth.

Without wasting any time, the farmer threw the young eagle up in the air. It flew just a few feet before crashing down to the ground like a chicken.

"I've lived all my life as a chicken. Even if what you're telling me is true, I'm not an eagle anymore," the eagle protested, deeply disappointed.

"Don't worry. Just keep trying, you will be proud of yourself," the farmer reassured him. As the day progressed, the young eagle could fly farther and farther. When the farmer was convinced that the young eagle was ready, he took the eagle to the edge of the highest point of the cliff.

The young eagle looked down the cliff and trembled. He'd never flown that high before. Maybe he would die. Maybe he should go back to the chickens.

"Don't look down," the farmer said. "Look up at the sky. Aim toward the sun. Have faith."

The young eagle lifted his sight, spread his wings, and the farmer let him go.

The farmer felt overwhelmed by emotion as he watched the majestic young eagle gliding and soaring effortlessly in the sky. Soon it was joined by another eagle. Together they soared and dived, playing the wind like a violin, and with the liberating sounds of screaming eagles, they disappeared into the horizons.

As the farmer stood there, gazing at the sky in awe, he knew, without a doubt, that he had done the right thing. He realized that helping the young eagle realize its true nature, to become who he was meant to be, was his greatest gift of love to the young eagle.

Are you an Eagle or Chicken?

A vital part of self-compassion is learning to listen to our hearts and ensure we don't allow fear or discouragement to force us to settle for less than the life we truly deserve, whether it is in our relationships, job, friends or other facets of life. There's a need for self-awareness, to know our true nature, to understand who we are, and to take actions that vitalize our essential nature. By taking a moment to review important areas of our life, such as personal relationship, friends, family, social, career, spirituality, physical and emotional well-being, we may detect areas where we need to take steps to liberate ourselves.

By Zeal Okogeri

42

A Simple
but Profound Phrase

Dr. Zeal Okogeri is one of the most spiritual friends I have, and he has provided me with an opportunity to leave my message in written form. I have decided to share my experience with the readers, especially with the Keio SFC basketball boys' team, which I have supervised for 24 years.

I have only two years left before I must retire from my current position as an English teacher and the head coach of the basketball team. I have been thinking deeply about what the most important thing for learners could possibly be. In other words, what important message can I possibly give to my students to always keep in mind? Putting aside knowledge, techniques for passing examinations, or advice on a way of life, what is it that young adults must not forget throughout their lives? As a life-long learner myself, there is a phrase that comes to mind, one that I will never forget, a phrase accidentally spoken to me more than 40 years ago by a kind, ordinary Japanese woman. Her message is what I will leave my students: "Making an effort, without doubt, is a valuable thing."

That utterance has remained very clear in my mind for more than 40 years. That is, even now, it is still alive, active, and effective in my life. It is not a proverb, nor a great man's maxim. An ordinary woman, whom I had never met, gave this priceless message to me in the elevator in Tokyo 40 years ago. Her words didn't seem to contain any pregnant meaning, nor have any connotations at all. It was a very straightforward expression. Everyone knows that the meaning of words can be changeable depending on the situation and the context. I have been wondering why her words had such an impact on me, enough to stay with me ever since, encouraging me to never quit in the quest to fulfill my dreams. Now I think that the answer may be due to the difficulties I was going through at that time.

Here is my story:

In March 1973, I moved to Tokyo from a small town in Fukuoka prefecture, in the northern part of Kyushu big island, Japan, to study at Waseda University. I was full of hope. However, at the same time, I was nervous about living in such a metropolitan place like Tokyo. Tokyo was too big a city for a country-folk like me.

Waseda is one of Japan's top private institutions of higher learning, which means the tuition was comparatively higher than that of state universities. It was not easy to live a comfortable life for students who were from provinces like mine. The cost of living—accommodation, food, clothing, and transportation—was high in Tokyo.

Before I applied for Waseda University, I knew it might be impossible to go to college in Tokyo. My father had fallen ill and couldn't work anymore. My family's economic situation was so deplorable that none of my five siblings could pursue higher education despite their excellent academic achievements. My father was not able to pay for my college expenses either.

That's why I decided to earn a living by delivering newspapers. I was attracted by an advertisement in the newspaper of a company that provided accommodation, breakfast, and dinner to student newspaper carriers. The ad said that the students only had to deliver the morning and evening papers in return for the company's shouldering all their school expenses. Although it was not an easy decision, I accepted the job, in case I passed the entrance examination to gain admission to Waseda University. I had applied to three universities at that time, including Hiroshima State University. However, before the results came out, I went ahead and contracted with the newspaper company. The news came that my name was on the list of successful applicants to Hiroshima University. When my brother telephoned me with the information, I had already started delivering newspapers to honor my commitment to the company in Shinjuku, Tokyo.

So, I started my life in Tokyo not as a college student, but as a working man. The working conditions were terrible, and the accommodation provided by the company was tiny. It was just a room measuring three tatami mats wide (2.7 x 1.8 meters) and equipped with a small desk and a bed. There was no bathroom in the room. This was not what I expected. We had to get up at 4:30 a.m. before sunrise every morning. I felt panic and terror because of the heavy workload.

I wanted to escape from this situation, but I knew it was impossible. I felt that I was wearing a chain around my ankles.

One day, I was so exhausted that, at dawn, I fell asleep and had a dream that my mother came to help me carry and deliver heavy newspapers. Then I was awakened by the loud noise of a delivery truck driver throwing bundles of papers from the loading platform. I wanted to leave this job and go back to my parents' home. Unfortunately, the contract stipulated that I must return all the money the company paid for my tuition if I quit the job before graduation. I had no choice but to carry out the duties. This was not a scholarship system but an education loan system. I was at a loss. I didn't know what to do. Discontent and frustration began to increase in my mind.

On the one hand, I wanted to master the job as soon as possible to make the working hours short and dissolve my frustration. But it was so difficult to deliver the paper to each customer's residence without making any mistakes. The company had imposed strict rules on newspaper carriers. For example, newspaper deliverers must not make noise during the early mornings so as not to disturb or wake up residents. I was careful not to make noise when I rode a bicycle or walked fast. Also, deliverers were not allowed to use elevators even if we were in a hurry. I had to climb the stairs on foot, even in high-rise buildings.

One day it was raining heavily. Weather was important because we had to finish delivering all morning newspapers to as many as 200 subscribers before they left for work. The bundle of newspapers, which included inserted supermarket advertisements, was so heavy. I had to be careful that rain did not damage the newspapers. Being in a big rush and panicking, I carried the heavy newspaper bundle on my bike. Unfortunately, I broke one of the rules and rode the elevator, feeling terrible. I was drenched from the rain. Water was dripping from my cap and raincoat. I thought no one would get on the elevator because it was so early in the morning. The elevator was moving upward to the floor I wanted to get off; unfortunately, it slowed down in transit. It was stopping on a different floor than I had intended. The door opened, and two middle-aged ladies stood in front of it. Our eyes met. One of the ladies frowned upon seeing me. My drenched clothes left her disgusted. However, the other lady smiled and said nothing. They got on the elevator. I felt it was taking forever for the elevator to reach my floor. I just looked up at the lighted display, which showed the number of each floor, without saying a word. The door opened, and when I got out of the elevator, the lady with a smile spoke to me: "Making an effort, without doubt, is a valuable thing."

I didn't respond, just mentally acknowledged what she had said, and left the elevator holding a bunch of newspapers. I began throwing newspapers into the slot of each room's door as quietly as possible. I didn't know who the lady in the elevator was, but she seemed to understand my situation by my appearance—a college student struggling to work his way through school. A few minutes after I heard her words, tears began flowing down my cheeks. Her warmhearted words moved me. I didn't know why I was encouraged so much by plain words like these. Probably, I felt lonely, and I needed someone to talk to. Afterward, I felt that all the discontent and frustration that had accumulated in my mind were dissolved. My heart was cheered, and I never thought that I had to withdraw from the university. I was grateful for the opportunity to meet her. I needed and appreciated the kind words of this stranger. Her words encouraged me to change my attitude toward myself and my situation.

Shortly after that incident, I was able to leave the newspaper company and move to the college dormitory. My second elder brother, who was working for the city hall of my hometown, offered to take care of my loan with the newspaper company. The living cost in the dormitory was low enough for me to pay for it by myself. I started several part-time jobs, such as tutoring, cleaning staff, factory work, and so on.

Since then, whenever I encountered hardship, I would recall the stranger's utterance, "Making an effort, without doubt, is a valuable thing." After I graduated from Waseda University with a degree in English language, I became an English teacher at a private high school. At first, I was not confident in terms of communicative English. I enrolled in a post-graduate program at Columbia University, Tokyo. I began studying TESOL (Teaching English to Speakers of Other Languages). It seemed impossible to attend this post-graduate course, spending all my Saturdays and Sundays along with teaching and coaching the basketball club. I nevertheless completed the program, but at a great cost to my health. Just before graduation, I was not able to finish my final thesis because I had developed liver cancer. On the advice of my doctor, I decided to forgo my graduation, although I had already spent a lot of money on tuition.

I was depressed again, not only about my situation but also my other siblings, who were also battling liver cancer. I asked for a second opinion from an herbalist, a Chinese medicine doctor. I was desperate and felt like I was trying to catch a straw while drowning in the river. My youngest brother passed away from cancer at the age of 39 years. He left behind a wife and a five-month-old daughter. My second eldest brother, who had shouldered my debt for the college expense, also died of cancer. My sister, two years younger than me, died of the same disease. She left a note for my brother minutes before her death, saying, "Thank you for coming to see me."

I thought I also had to prepare for death. Again, that phrase appeared in my mind, "Making an effort, without doubt, is a valuable thing." However, this time, the expression seemed superficial to me because of the sadness I was going through.

After the funerals of my brothers and sister, I began to think about how much time I had. "How long could I live from now?" Yes, I felt that death was the starting line. "What could I do until I passed away?" I found this way of thinking to be positive. Then I recalled the magic phrase again. This time I agreed with my modified version: "Making an effort until the end is beautiful." That phrase cheered me up, and I tried to take any chances I could to live for other people.

Strangely, my health suddenly became better. The results of my annual health check showed no problems, so I could continue to work.

In 2008, I got a chance to study abroad for one year, thanks to the exchange program between Keio University and the University of Hawaii at Manoa. I had many experiences there. It is in Hawaii that I met Dr. Zeal Okogeri. By chance, I also met Troy Fernandez and Jake Shimabukuro, who are superb ukulele players. I learned how to play some beautiful pieces of music from Troy. I took them into my English class and taught the students how enjoyable it is to sing English songs while playing the ukulele. I joined the Honolulu Marathon and became a finisher. I coached basketball, telling the boys to achieve their goals at their own pace, not only in basketball but also in academics. I made some nice friends there, one of whom was a spiritual person who instructed me, "Take a chance any time." All of these were unexpected, beautiful experiences.

I took another chance to study abroad. From 2011 to 2012, I attended graduate school at the University of Michigan and earned a Master of Arts degree.

Looking back on my life and career, I never thought I would have succeeded in following these academic paths since my graduation from Waseda University. Neither did I think I would survive liver cancer. Without the kind and moving words of the woman in the elevator, I don't think I would have galvanized the strength to pull through my illness, or to accomplish my dreams. Even though I'm already 63 years old, I'm planning to take on some new challenges. When my teaching and coaching job ends in two years, I'm looking forward to embarking on some adventures. This way, when the basketball team members come to visit me in the future, I'll have plenty of good stories to share with them.

By Takumi Tanabe

43

Teenaged Saving Grace

All I ever wanted to be was a teacher. After several years of following all the necessary steps to become a certified teacher in Oklahoma, my hard work paid off. I received a position at the same middle school I had attended in my hometown, where I taught alongside a few of my former teachers. I never understood what "coming full circle" meant until then.

I began my first-year teaching English to seventh-grade students, and many people warned me about the "rough age." One teacher even told me during my orientation that it was okay to cry. Though this only slightly worried me, I steeled myself with the romantic notions of reaching every student in a meaningful way and my students leaving my classroom with full knowledge of each day's lesson.

From Day One, the surprises kept rolling in. My students were on different levels academically; therefore, I was lucky if half of my students understood what I was saying, much less teaching. Some of the students had parents who didn't care. Once that happens, a child is lost, and it's hard to convince them that school is important.

And the work was never done. No matter how many

photocopies were made, papers graded, parents called, forms completed, lessons planned, and trash cans emptied, there was still more to do. It was, by far, the most stressful job I ever had.

The biggest surprise, the one thing I never saw coming was how cold and indifferent the other teachers were toward me. At first, I thought it was simply newbie awkwardness, so I joined their conversations at lunch and in the hallways after school to break the ice. Every encounter was the same. Backs were turned, gazes fixed on each other, and the undeniable sense that I wasn't welcomed. I tried a different approach and began stocking my classroom mini fridge with a variety of sodas. I let the teachers come into my room and take them as they pleased. I baked cookies and bread, packaged them beautifully, and gave them away individually with heartfelt notes of praise or encouragement. Nothing changed. I was an outsider.

The teacher I met in orientation was right. I did cry—a lot. But not because of the students. I had never been in a more lonesome workplace, and I craved my old job, where my coworkers were a second family. I couldn't figure out why I was ignored. My mom believed it was because I was young, unmarried, without kids, and attractive. Though they would never have known, I was heartbroken.

I prayed continuously for God to send me a friend, someone to show me kindness, and to make my presence feel wanted. God has an interesting way of answering prayers. He gives us what we seek in a way we would never have thought of ourselves.

Students began bringing me gifts, such as decorations for my classroom, inspirational decor for my home, homemade cookies and muffins, books I had wanted to read, and a variety of artwork they had created for me. During this time, I had taught my students to practice gratitude journaling, a daily exercise I had been doing on my own for over a year. They wrote three things they were grateful for every day and an explanation of why. I picked them up every other week to read.

Much to my surprise, many of my students wrote that they were grateful for having me as their teacher. Their words brought tears to my eyes. Some of their passages read, "Miss Smart is very encouraging, and she has faith in everyone. One thing that I love about her is that she sees the best in people, no matter what," and "Miss Smart has inspired me to do more. I know that her purpose in life is to inspire people and to make them believe in themselves," and lastly, "I like how Miss Smart opens up to us more than most teachers. She also introduced us to 'the grateful notebook.' It makes me appreciate the little things in life I never noticed."

If all this wasn't enough to open my eyes to the radiating warmth and kindness of my 12- and 13-year-old students, it was when my student Kaylee came up to me one day in the hall, wrapped her arms around me, and whispered, "I love you" that I knew God had answered my prayer in a most beautiful way. It was the first of many hugs and words of endearment from students.

For the rest of the year, many students visited my classroom after school to help clean the floor and desks, receive advice on keeping true friends, and be comforted when life's burdens became too much to bear. All this was far greater than exchanging empty conversations with adults who didn't care to know me.

They don't know it, but those students were my saving grace. If not for their generous and loving hearts, I would have quit before the end of the school year. Any time I hear now of a teacher going into middle school, I think about how fortunate they are and how blessed their life will become.

By Haylie Smart

44

A Kiss from Grace

I think that sometimes kindness by its very nature comes when we least expect it. Maybe that's part of its role: to wake us up from our illusion.

When I was a teenager, I lived in the suburbs of Toronto, Canada. The population was booming and the roads were typical of any suburban road near a major urban center: too busy.

One day I was leaving work and needed to make it home in time to grab a quick bite before yoga class that evening. However, I was facing the very real risk of missing the class since a client had kept me back about 15 minutes, and it was rush hour, and my instructor didn't accept people who were not punctual. I felt a lot of stress about 'making life decisions' at that time, and felt that I needed that class to relax. Despite telling myself to calm down, there was a growing sense of urgency inside of me to get home. When I finally made it out the door and into my car, I pulled out of my office parking lot and onto Fisherman's Drive. This is a deceptive name, as nothing about the street is reminiscent of a small fishing village unless you were to take into account its size. Instead, it is a narrow access point to a commercial and light industrial business park. Unfortunately for those in a hurry, this small street can take up to five minutes until the green points in our direction.

It is safe to say that I was not feeling patient that day as I looked at the clock multiple times – per minute – waiting for the light to turn.

Thump thump. Thump thump.

I could hear my heart.

My mind was analytical and time-pressed, far from the state of peace I was rushing toward.

Thump thump. Thump thump.

Then it happened.

The light turned the most glorious shade of green, as bright as a glowing beacon of hope shining from above. A feeling of joy arose as I thought, 'Maybe I can make it in time.'

Thump thump. Thump thump.

But nothing happened.

That is to say, the car in front of me did not budge one inch. My joy quickly turned. My ill temperament started to gain momentum when the couple in front of me blatantly ignored the extremely small window of opportunity and started to kiss.

Thump thump. Thump thump.

Now, as upset as I was for my completely selfish reasons, I still thought it was sweet.

Thump thump. Thump thump.

Then another thing happened.

A driver ran the red light at a breakneck speed.

Thump thump. Thump thump.

The people in the car held a loving gaze.

Thump thump. Thump thump.

The people in front of me casually moved into the

intersection, seemingly unaware of the near miss.

Thump thump. Thump thump.

I watched without moving.

Thump thump. Thump thump.

HONK!! HOOONK!!

The person behind me, perhaps also unaware, was impatient just as I had been only a few heartbeats before.

Thump thump. Thump thump.

I took a deep breath and moved into the intersection, thanking the beauty that caused those two souls to choose that moment to kiss, letting their bubble of love shelter who knows how many people from a potentially fatal accident. For all I know, this was a secret only I was let in on.

Even though this was almost 20 years ago, the lesson to trust the benevolence of timing has stuck with me.

Today, if I miss a train or cannot find my keys, or if for some unknown reason my phone will not turn on before an important meeting, I remember to take a deep breath and listen to my beating heart. If I can turn up the volume on my inner wisdom, it is sure to remind me that whatever I think is so important to rush for does not really matter. After all, who knows why it is perfect for me to arrive when I arrive?

By Adrienne McCurdy

45

You Have Nothing to Be Ashamed Of

One morning I awoke and heard the still small voice inside urging me to drive into town to meet some friends for lunch. Over the years, I have learned to trust my intuition and to act on these nudges, so I got ready and headed out.

Being that it was a Saturday, the restaurant where I met my friends was bustling and crowded. Before we were seated, I decided to use the restroom. While waiting in a long line, I noticed a lovely middle-aged woman standing at the sink area, looking bewildered.

She stepped toward me and some other women in line as if trying to get our attention, all the while digging frantically through her large handbag.

I could see the discomfort on the women's faces. Suspicious of her intentions, the ladies averted their eyes, avoiding direct contact with her. As her eyes met mine, she pulled a card from her purse and held it up to me. The card read, "I had a stroke. Will you please help me?"

"Sure, I would be happy to help you," I said. She appeared to be experiencing cognitive challenges due to her stroke, and she required assistance washing and drying her hands.

As I pumped soap from the dispenser into her open hand, she looked up at me tearfully, like a lost child, and said in slurred speech, "I am so ashamed."

I saw that this shame came from a deep feeling of helplessness. It was clear that this experience had altered her life and identity, greatly restricting her independence, her confidence, and the basic abilities that most of us take for granted each day.

I looked into her eyes and heard myself say, "You have nothing to be ashamed of. You are loved." The words did not come from me, but through me, and carried a power that moved both of us.

She began to tremble and tears ran down her cheeks. I put my arm around her shoulder and we embraced. I felt a current of divine, unconditional love flow between us. In that instant, we shared an understanding that transcended words.

Later, while washing my hands at the sink, I noticed a woman staring at me who had been in the same line. After a moment or two she said, "I have to tell you. Earlier today I was wondering if there were any good people left in the world. Then I saw what you did for that woman. You renewed my faith in humanity."

I stood in awe of what had just occurred. How easily could I have missed this opportunity had I not listened to my inner voice. This experience was a testament to the power of love, which is expressed through small acts of kindness. It also confirmed that the still, small voice within is, at its essence, LOVE. When I am willing to listen to it, I find myself in alignment with the Divine.

By Silana Lundin

46

One Hardboiled Egg

My mother, Elizabeth Moore Arlen, shared this story with me, an experience she had while serving the troops and their families.

In the early 1940's, during World War II, she was a student at Barnard College in New York City. She and many other women donated their time working at a food kitchen set up for feeding the troops. The kitchen was sponsored by the recently formed USO (United Service Organizations), which provided a wide variety of programs and services to support the morale, welfare, and recreational needs of U.S. troops and their families. Because food was so scarce, the women would use eggs donated by local residents to make large amounts of egg salad. People in the community were asked to donate fresh eggs for this effort.

One day, a humbly dressed woman came in with a small basket, asking to donate a single hardboiled egg. One of the other female volunteers told her it was too late to donate for that day and that they accepted only fresh eggs. As the dejected women turned to leave, Mom intervened by taking her arm and gently escorting her off to the side. Mom told her that she would be delighted to accept the egg and told her how incredibly grateful she was for this generous donation.

The next day, the same women came back to the USO kitchen. She expressed interest in making a donation, but said she would speak only with my mom. When Mom greeted her, the woman told Mom that the single egg was a test. She had heard of the recently formed USO program, but wanted to make sure that her donation would be appreciated and go to the right person or organization.

She thanked Mom for her kindness and handed her a donation check made out to the USO for $15,000 – in today's dollars, that check would be worth $227,000! Mom handed the check to her superior and never said another word about it. In fact, I found out yesterday that I am the only one in the family she ever told this story to. That was Mom: kind, selfless, and giving, with amazing grace.

by Ken Arlen

Chapter Seven

YOU CAN NEVER GO WRONG BY BEING KIND

One of the most difficult things to give away is kindness, it usually comes back to you.

—Anonymous

47

Every Act of Love
Makes a Difference

Every so often, when we consider making a difference in the world, in our country, our communities, or our families, the problems we are trying to fix are so complex and overwhelming that we don't know where to start. Think about the number of people who are homeless. Think about the millions of young people who are alcoholics and drug addicts. Think about abused women. Think about human trafficking. Think about racism, abandoned children, poverty, dysfunctional families, gay and lesbian issues, religious fanaticism, terrorism, and so on. How are you going to begin to solve the problems of the world and make it a better place?

Frankly, when you think about this seriously, the weight can be so heavy that you don't even want to carry it in your mind, let alone try to fix it. Besides, you have your problems to deal with.

What we often forget is that every little act of love makes a big difference. We don't have to solve the entire problem. If we can do what we can, that will make a significant difference in the lives of so many people. Even if you were able to make a difference in just one person's life, you would have made a considerable contribution, for, without you, that person might not receive assistance.

I was fortunate to come across a magnificent story that you may have already heard. This story is worth retelling because it demonstrates that every little thing we do for the benefit of another matter:

At the first glimmer of light of dawn in a distant Pacific island, a young man walked at the edge of the seashore. There had been an unusual storm the night before, and he knew this would be a good morning to find seashells. With pants rolled up above his ankles, he walked along, looking down for what treasures he might find.

Then, the young man looked up and could barely make out a figure of an old man ahead of him. The young man watched as the old man bent down to pick up an object from the sand and toss it into the surf. As he got closer, and the light of morning began to turn the sand pink, he noticed that the old man was picking up starfish that had been tossed up on the beach by the storm. Thousands of them had filled the sand, but one by one, the old man was picking them up and tossing them back into the surf.

Nearing the old man, the young man introduced himself, and said, "Excuse me, sir. I have been watching you from a distance for the last half hour. Do you realize how many starfishes are out here? Even if you manage to save one hundred of them, what difference would that make? Thousands would still die."

The old man smiled compassionately and looked at the young boy, then picked up another starfish. As he gently tossed it back into the surf, he said to the young boy, "I certainly made a difference to that one, didn't I, son?"

The old man did make a difference, just as you and I can make a difference wherever we are.

Let us not allow the enormity of our world problems to overwhelm us. Simply identify an area where you can be useful and do what you can. For example, you can telephone someone you've not spoken to in a while, perhaps your parents, grandparents, siblings, or friends. Many people are quietly battling loneliness or some sort of health problem and wish someone would reach out to them and see how they are doing. It makes a huge difference to have companionship or to know that somebody cares when you're feeling neglected or forgotten. Making a phone call or paying a visit to someone you love or someone you know who is going through a rough time can be truly life-enhancing. Often, we assume that people in our lives are doing fine. But they may not! They may just be keeping their problems to themselves, like many people do. So, don't assume everything is fine, call and say hello. Ask how things are going. Sometimes, all a person needs is for their existence to be acknowledged, and that will keep them going for a while.

There are many simple ways to uplift those around us. Sometimes we think that we must wait until we can make a major impact. What we often don't realize is that, in the final analysis, it is the little things that we do in life that matter so much. It is our thoughtful involvement with our family, friends, and neighbors that add meaning to life. It is also our gifts of kindness and generosity to people that we don't even know that sustains life itself.

By Zeal Okogeri

48

The Gift
Of a Lifetime

When I was one year old, our family moved to, of all places, Calcutta, India. My father, James Villemonte, was a professor of Civil Engineering at the University of Wisconsin in Madison. Through an offer from the university, he had accepted an assignment to the Bengal Engineering College in Calcutta to help develop a new postgraduate program. He was part of a team of six professors and their families.

At the college in India, our family lived on campus in a simple apartment. The college also provided servants to help us with daily duties like cooking, cleaning, laundry, etc. My mother remembered the day when she and Dad went to select the servants who would be helping us. All the professors and their wives gathered at a place where the prospects were waiting to be chosen. They were of all ages, but mostly on the younger side. They were poor, and being picked certainly meant a better life for the next few years for them and their families.

During the selection process, mom said that my dad chose the oldest servant to sweep for us. Later, Mom asked him why he had chosen an old man when so many robust young men were available. "Because I knew that nobody else would choose him," Dad said. This man's name was Ghulam, and it would not be the last time he would be the recipient of a kind deed from my parents.

After three years, we left India in 1958 and returned home to America. The assignment my father was involved in at the college was a big success, and Indian students from there started coming over to America to get their doctorates. Many came to the university in Madison. I know that my father was fulfilled from the assignment in India and was grateful no harm came to his family during the experience.

In 1978, 20 years after we had left, Mom and Dad decided to go back to India to visit the college and see how things were going. One day, while they were walking on the campus, my mom saw an elderly gentleman slowly coming their way. As the man got closer, she whispered to Dad, "Jimmy, I think that's Ghulam!" Indeed, it was!

They stopped and greeted him. It seemed that Ghulam had learned to speak a little English, so my dad started to talk to him to find out how he was doing. And, yes, after a little bit, he did remember them. He was shocked to see them again after so many years. As they talked, my dad, as was his nature, tried to figure out a way to help Ghulam—and in a way that Ghulam could accept.

During their time living amongst the Indian people, my parents had found that they are very proud people and not likely to accept a sudden handout of cash for no reason. So, on the spot, my dad served up a little story to Ghulam that wasn't true, but that certainly served his purpose admirably at that moment.

"Ghulam," my dad said, "What a good fortune it is to meet you here like this, for this gives me the opportunity to take care of something that has been bothering me since the day we left, all those 20 years ago."

"You see, Ghulam," he continued, "twenty years ago, we had so much going on, getting our things ready to leave and all, that I later realized I had forgotten to pay you your last month's wages! Now, with meeting you here today, I can finally take care of this, and everything will be settled. And, of course, there is the matter of interest added to the sum over the 20 years, so I will include that in the final amount that you are due."

My mom said that Ghulam was very surprised at this, but in the end, he accepted Dad's story and seemed visibly moved by the sudden appearance of this unexpected money into his life. After a few silent moments, he said, "Mr. and Mrs. Villemonte, as you can see, I am a very old man and will die soon. Being a Muslim, it has always been a dream of mine since I was a young man to one day visit the Holy City, Mecca. But I have always been too poor to do so. But now, with this money, I can finally go there, fulfill my dream, and be able to die in peace."

Wow, a man being able to die in peace and fulfill a life-long dream simply because of a gift of kindness given at a chance meeting. My mom and dad could just as easily have greeted Ghulam, wished him well, and then walked on. And yet, I think my dad sensed that a special opportunity had arrived at this chance meeting during which he could truly help this person. And so, Dad went one step further and devised a way to give this man some extra funds that enabled him to fulfill a life-long dream.

It made me think: "How many times have I had the opportunity to help someone but didn't?" "How many times did I hesitate to help because I thought it wouldn't matter?" Then I thought about Ghulam and the gift of love he received from my father. That precious opportunity to uplift an elderly man, a devoted Muslim, by helping him fulfill his religious duty, would have been lost if my father had hesitated to give.

When we decide to give, we may never know how our gifts of kindness may help another, and who knows, we just might be giving someone the gift of a lifetime.

By John Villemonte

49

Keep the Distance Small

There's a story about a Hindu saint who was visiting the River Ganges to take a bath. On the banks he found a group of family members shouting in anger at each other. He turned to his disciples, smiled, and asked, "Why do people shout in anger at each other?"

The disciples thought for a while. One of them said, "Because we lose our calm, we shout."

"But why should you shout when the other person is right next to you? You can just as well tell him what you have to say in a soft manner," said the saint.

The disciples gave some other answers but none satisfied them. Finally, the saint explained, "When two people are angry at each other, their hearts are distant. To cover that distance, they must shout to be able to hear each other. The angrier they are, the stronger they will have to shout to hear each other to cover that great distance.

"What happens when two people fall in love? They don't shout at each other but talk softly, because their hearts are very close. The distance between them is either nonexistent or very small."

The saint continued. "When they love each other even more, what happens? They do not speak, only whisper, and they get even closer to each other in their love. Finally, they do not even need to whisper; they only look at each other and that's all. That is how close two people are when they love each other."

He looked at his disciples and said, "So, when you argue, do not let your hearts get distant, do not say words that distance each other more, or else there will come a day when the distance is so great that you will not find the path to return."

By Anonymous

50

The Richest Man
In the World

The more we practice kindness and compassion, the more we open our hearts to love. It's like storing up the most precious treasures for ourselves. Here is a story about the richest man in the world:

There was a king who lived in an ancient city. He was the richest man in the world. He owned practically everything. One of his advisors was an exceptionally compassionate saint who taught and demonstrated love, kindness, and compassion to the people. Because love was part of his essential nature, he was respected, trusted, and profoundly admired by the people.

The saint had the gift of prophecy. Whenever he had a dream, it came true. This made him indispensable to the king, who wanted to know many things to help him rule his kingdom.

One day, the saint woke up in the wee hours of the morning with a most disturbing dream. He rushed to the palace to see the king. "What brought you here so early in the morning?" demanded the king. "Your Highness, I am so sorry to tell you this, but last night I dreamed that the richest man in the world will die tomorrow," the saint solemnly replied.

The king was shocked because he was the richest man in the world. Trying to conceal his fear, he laughed jovially and asked, "Is that all? Don't worry about me, dear friend. I am healthy, and I've never felt better in my life."

"Fine, sir," responded the saint. "I just wanted to notify you of my dream, as I have always done in the past." He left and returned to the small, modest church where he lived.

As the king went about his day, he kept thinking about the saint's dream. The saint had never been wrong. Concerned, the king summoned the best doctors in the kingdom to his palace, to give him a complete evaluation. Although he received a clean bill of health from the doctors, the king was still worried. He went through the rest of the day, expecting the worst. At night, he was afraid to fall asleep, for he feared he might not wake to see the next day.

As luck would have it, the king was alive and well the next morning. Full of excitement and pride for having beaten the saint's prophecy, the king put on his best royal robe and eagerly strolled outside his palace with his entourage. He wanted to assure his people that he was alive and well because news about the saint's dreadful dream had spread all over the kingdom. But when the king stepped out of the palace gates, the most unusual sight was waiting for him; thousands of his people were weeping and throwing themselves on the ground. The screams of hysteria, anguished crying, and fearful prayers of the crowd touched the king very deeply. Moved that his subjects were mourning his death, he raised his right hand in the air and shouted, "Stop it! Stop it! Don't cry anymore; I'm alive! I'm alive!" But the hysterical crowd ignored him completely.

Bewildered, the king called on one of the mourners to find out what was going on.

It was at this time that the king learned the saint had died.

And here was the king thinking he was the richest man in the world.

By Zeal Okogeri

51

Peace Starts in the Family

The topic of kindness is very close to my heart, so I would like to write about it through three important experiences from my life. Each in its own way has taught me the value of kindness. Each also made me realize that kindness doesn't need to be reserved for only human beings. The warm blanket of kindness must be extended to all sentient beings on this earth.

Let me start by introducing myself. My name is Konchog Tobden. I am a Buddhist monk born and raised in a small rural village in southern India. Currently I am completing a master's program in Buddhist studies (MBuddhStud) at the University of Hong Kong. Growing up, I didn't have any memory of my mother because she passed away when I was very young. I believe that mothers in general are the epitome of kindness. However, I'm lucky in that I had my father around when I was growing up; he showered me with all the love and kindness I needed, and I love him for that. As I grew up, I realized that his kindness extended to everyone around him. He is a soft-spoken person, kind in heart and helpful to anyone who needs it. That made me see him in a whole new light and now I love him more than ever. I also respect him a lot as a human being. His actions and principles formed the foundation of my own philosophy in life. I read a quote somewhere that peace starts from the basic level of family and then moves up the chain to the highest level of society. In this regard, I've been lucky to have a kind, supportive, and loving father. He sowed a seed of kindness in my heart that I've been nurturing throughout my life.

The second experience that further strengthens my belief in kindness was through my education. At an early age, I became a Buddhist monk, and our monastery provided me with everything, from food, shelter, and clothing to education. I learned to read and write Tibetan, as well as about ritual prayers and advanced studies in philosophy for 13 years. Throughout my years as a student, I learned Buddhist philosophy, which has kindness and compassion as its core value. I was imparted with these valuable lessons under the guidance of kindhearted teachers. Day in and day out, I learned the importance of kindness and compassion in our daily lives for the good of the whole universe. We have daily prayer rituals, a part of which includes kindness toward and wellbeing for all sentient beings. Regardless of your animosity toward other people, a Buddhist always prays for everyone, from a small ant to the largest mammal, for we all desire happiness and peace. Each and every one on this planet deserves our kindness and compassion. In addition, we believe in the reincarnation process, which means that we have been through the life cycle numerous times in the past. Someone who is an enemy in this life may have been our loved one in the past. That's why you should show to everyone the same respect and kindness you would show to your own parents. By reading texts from Buddhist scriptures, especially the book by the Indian guru Shanti Deva, called Bodhisattvacharyavatara, I have turned around my life for the good and am able to tackle negative feelings like envy, jealousy, and greed on a day-to-day basis. Books such as this guide us toward liberating ourselves with kindness and compassion.

Last of all, I would like to emphasize the role of my spiritual masters. I wholeheartedly admire and follow His Holiness the 14th Dalai Lama, His Holiness the 17th Karmapa, His Holiness Drikung Kyabgyon Chetsang and Chutsang, His Eminence Ayang Rinpoche, and Kyabje Drubwang Pema Norbu Rinpoche. I have been studying and following their teachings for as long as I can remember. Each of them in their own way promotes peace and harmony in the world. I believe that their teachings have collectively made me a better person. Their extremely vast source of kindness has already helped many people on this earth and they are continuing to work toward a better world. Considering the limited scope of this article, I will write only about the influence of His Holiness the Dalai Lama. It's beyond the scope of this writing and well beyond my limited knowledge to properly explain the teachings of His Holiness. However, I'll try to do so through one of his two famous commitments. He has committed his whole life to the promotion of basic human value and religious harmony. He believes that everyone on this planet deserves kindness, compassion, tolerance, and so on. If everyone has kindness and compassion as their basic human value, as their core principle, most of the problems faced by the human population can be resolved. In this time and era, people are focused on self-interest and they sacrifice others for their own gain. This only leads to more problems down the line. It is vital to share and promote kindness and peace around you. As I mentioned earlier, peace and kindness start spreading from the family, the household, to the highest levels of society. The same is true of anger and hatred.

In conclusion, I would like to remind anyone who is reading what little I have to offer that kindness is not a destination. It's a process and a journey that you should keep practicing on a day-to-day basis. Go out there in the world and spread kindness and compassion to all. It can be as small as giving up your seat on a crowded train, giving a kind smile to a stranger, or building a shelter for the homeless. No task is too small when it comes to a kind act. I would like to end by leaving you with His Holiness the Dalai Lama's quote: "My religion is very simple. My religion is kindness."

By Konchog Tobden

52

Watch Out for Distractions

There's a marvelous story about a gifted, but poor candle maker. For a long time, he struggled to turn his candle-making business into a profitable venture. Finally he turned to God, asking for help to better care for his family. Not long after his plea, a friend came to his house with the most incredible news. He told the candle maker about a distant island that was saturated with diamonds. Anyone could go there and take as many diamonds as they desired.

The candle maker was absolutely excited, but felt the news sounded too good to be true. "There must be a catch to this," he said, scratching his head.

"Well, yes," replied his friend. "There is a catch. The island can only be reached by boat, and the only boat that sails there travels just once every seven years. Now, if you're interested, you better pack your bags right away because it just happens that the boat is leaving tomorrow."

Not wanting to miss an opportunity of a lifetime, the candle maker talked the situation over with his family, promising that if all goes well, their lives would forever change for the better.

The next day, he was on his way to board the boat. Everyone wished him a safe and successful journey and looked forward to the riches he would bring back.

When the candle maker reached the island, he realized that his friend wasn't kidding. There were precious stones glittering everywhere. Diamonds were so plentiful, like sand on the beach, that the local residents ignored them. And since there was no law against collecting them, the candle maker brought out his large bag and began to help himself. Just then, he heard a voice: "What are you doing gathering those useless stones?" He looked up and saw a native of the island looking down at him.

"These stones are not useless," protested the candle marker. "They're real diamonds and I'm taking them home." "Fine," replied the stranger. "But have you forgotten you can't return home for at least seven years? How do you intend to feed yourself in the meantime?" The candle maker suddenly realized there was no need to pack diamonds yet. He could collect them whenever he wanted because of the sheer abundance.

Since the only trade he knew was candle making, he decided to try his trade and see if he would making enough money to keep himself going for the next seven years. Surprisingly, within just a few months, he became one of the most popular residents in the island. The islanders loved and praised his work. He couldn't make enough candles to keep up with demands.

For the first time in his life, the candle maker felt significant. He thought he finally made it big. By the time seven years passed and he was ready to sail home, he was so consumed by public adoration that he forgot why he came to the island in the first place. When the boat came, the man boarded the boat with bags filled with candles. Upon his return, his family and friends excitedly rushed to see the diamonds but were utterly disappointed to find bags of candles.

We become like the candle maker when we allow anyone or anything to cause us to drift away from our mission or purpose.

By Zeal Okogeri

52

The Gifts
Of Meditation

What would be the best message or story that I could share with you, the reader, as this book is coming to a close? After much consideration, I asked myself, "What is the greatest gift you've received in this lifetime for your personal growth?" The answer was easy, meditation! So, I'm going to share my story of discovering a most transformative mantra meditation. No other tool or technique has transformed my life, like the daily practice of meditation. It allowed me to connect within and recognize the relentless generosities of Spirit in my life. Through meditation, I've been blessed with unique skills for navigating my life and for helping others. The book you're reading now, for example, is a natural byproduct of years of meditation.

The benefits of meditation are many. I'll mention just a few. Please keep in mind that certain specific benefits derived from meditation depend on the type of meditation you practice. Meditation can improve your overall health, reduce stress, help you connect better with yourself and others, sharpen your focus, increase attention and intuition, and help you be yourself. It can help reduce mental chatter and improve your ability to remain calm under pressure. It can help you become more aware of your destructive self-talk; this way, you can start practicing self-talk that is much kinder and compassionate. The daily practice of meditation gives you inner strength and resilience; and provides spiritual protection and guidance. Lastly, meditation helps you become wiser.

There is a wide range of contemplative practices available from the world's great spiritual traditions, such as mantra meditation, mindfulness, guided, visualization, watching thoughts, breathing, walking meditation, and many more. The key is to find one that resonates with you. And once you find one that you like, you need to practice consistently and relentlessly. That means making time to meditate every day, without skipping a day! If you already meditate daily, congratulations! But if you're new to meditation, it is wise to find an experienced, reliable, and kind teacher to guide you and make sure you are practicing correctly. And once you've mastered the technique, you can move on and practice on your own.

For many years, I practiced the breathing and silent meditation until I discovered mantra meditation through a chance meeting in Marina Del Rey, Los Angeles, California.

It was in the spring of 1990 when I decided to leave New Jersey and relocate to California. I had visited Los Angeles the year before and was pleased with the weather, as well as the liberal attitude of Californians.

In L.A., I stayed with a friend in Marina Del Rey until I could organize myself. I liked Marina Del Rey. Santa Monica, Beverly Hills, and Venice Beach were nearby. There were plenty of activities, such as bicycling, boating, jogging, and enjoying a variety of street performances at Venice Beach. Since I didn't have friends other than my host, I decided to get more socially involved.

Luckily, I picked up the local paper and saw a listing for Toastmasters International, a public speaking organization. The group was meeting at a restaurant within walking distance of where I lived, and it was open, at no cost, to anyone who wanted to attend.

"Perfect," I said.

I walked to the meeting that evening. About 20 Toastmasters were present. I was warmly welcomed and was later invited to give an introductory speech. I was nervous about speaking in front of a group of strangers. The last talk I had given in college was a total disaster. I was so nervous that, to this day, I don't remember how I concluded my presentation. This time, though, I managed to wing it. After my speech, there was uproarious cheering and clapping. They had apparently enjoyed it. I couldn't believe it. "Maybe they were just being kind to me," I thought. But after the meeting, half of the attendees gathered around me and told me how much they enjoyed my brief speech. This time I thought, "Maybe they did enjoy my presentation." I was encouraged.

As an aside, I would highly recommend joining Toastmasters to anyone interested in improving their oral presentation and leadership skills. It is perhaps the most cost-effective and supportive way of developing confidence and becoming proficient in public speaking. To locate a Toastmasters club near you in any part of the world, you can visit: www.toastmasters.org

As I continued talking with the friendly members of Toastmasters, the crowd dwindled until I was left talking with a middle-aged, red-haired woman who took a special interest in me, wanting to know everything about me. Our conversation quickly moved on to the topic of spirituality, and we had a wonderful time sharing our mutual interest in personal development. A few days later, she invited me to a meditation session with her group at a center in Santa Monica.

There were about 25 people who gathered for the meditation practice. I was about to experience, for the first time, a mantra meditation practice called the HU chant, HU song, or HU mantra. Before starting the spiritual exercise, the facilitator provided a general introduction.

He said that the HU mantra had been practiced for thousands of years to attune oneself to the presence of God. It is the primordial sound current or the all-pervasive universal consciousness within everyone. This exercise allows the practitioner to have direct experiences with the twin aspects of the Holy Spirit—the light and sound current of God. It has the power to heal, give insight, balance life, protect, and uplift the practitioner spiritually.

He said that the sacred word 'HU' pronounced Hue, is an ancient name for God, and a love song to God. In reciting HU, you are essentially submitting to the Will of God, meaning that you agree to step aside, to get out of the way, and allow the Divine to arrange your life in the best way possible. In doing so, you are welcoming the gifts of Spirit into your life. And each time you chant HU, you are renewing your commitment to let go and let God. In other words, you are saying, "Not My Will, But May Thy Will Be Done."

He explained that the simplicity of this ancient spiritual exercise makes it appealing to people of all backgrounds. Anyone, regardless of background or beliefs, can practice the

HU. It does not interfere with your faith but allows for greater awareness. Like other meditation practices, consistency is essential. You can begin by reciting HU for just ten minutes, twice per day, and increase the duration gradually to allow yourself enough time to assimilate the vibration. Eventually, you can increase the duration to 20 minutes, twice per day, to reap the many benefits of this practice. HU can be practiced alone or in a group. It can be recited silently or out loud.

At this point, he asked everyone to get comfortable in their seats. "Sit with your back straight, feet planted on the floor, and your hands resting comfortably on your lap. Put your attention gently on the spot between your eyebrows, also referred to as 'spiritual eye.' Then, in a long, drawn-out breath, simply sing or chant, HU-U-U-U-U-U." While chanting, listen to the sound you're producing. If your mind wanders, gently bring it back to the sound of HU.

After we chanted for about 20 minutes, he said in a soft voice, "May the Blessing Be!" Then he instructed everyone to keep their eyes closed and go into silent contemplation. After about three minutes, he said, "You may open your eyes when you are ready."

When I opened my eyes, I knew, without a doubt, that I had just received one of the most precious gifts of this lifetime. The divine melody evoked my spirit! I felt my body pulsating. I felt happier and peaceful.

Before we left the meditation gathering, the facilitator said, "If you ever want to experience love, all you need to do is ask. Sing HU and ask God to show you love."

A few weeks later, I remembered what the facilitator said, and before I went to sleep, I sang HU for about 10 minutes, after which I said inwardly, "God, show me, Love." That night I had an exceptional dream experience. In my dream, I was cheerfully walking on a beautiful summer day. A short distance away stood a beautiful large tree with lush branches and leaves. It was a rather unusual tree. Except for the trunk, the entire tree was bright white. It looked like a tree that was freshly covered by snow during the winter. However, when I got closer, I realized that the tree was actually covered by a large group of tiny white birds. They were the smallest birds I had ever seen. Because of their size, there must have been thousands of them on the tree. Careful not to alarm the birds, I gently climbed the tree, found a spot on a branch, and sat down. Then I reached out and gently captured one of the little birds. I was curious about why they were so small. When the other birds realized what I had just done, they all flew away from the tree, leaving it bare, though they all continued hovering around the tree. Intuitively, I knew they were wondering what I intended to do with their friend that I was holding in my hands.

I examined the little bird in my hands with wonder, looking at every part of its intricate design with amazement. Then I opened my hands and let it go. It flew high in the sky and joyfully joined its friends. What happened next was something I never anticipated. Filled with gratitude that I had released one of them, the entire group of birds came and landed on me, from head to toe. There was no spot on my body that was not covered by these tiny white birds, and the birds that couldn't find space to land on my body layered on top of each other. The intensity of love that I felt pouring upon me from these birds was so overwhelming that, in the dream, I began weeping tears of joy. I just couldn't handle the immensity of God's love. It was way too much for me. In fact, when I woke up from the dream, tears were flowing down my face. So, while I was experiencing this overwhelming love in the dream state, my physical body was being moved by the experience. I realized then that chanting HU is indeed a love song to God. HU has the capacity to spiritualize one's consciousness and blow the heart wide open.

I have since been practicing the HU spiritual exercise for more than 25 years and have been sharing it with others. HU has helped me develop more love, kindness, strength, inner peace, and some unique skills. I'm deeply grateful for the gifts of the Light and Sound Current meditation.

With Blessing,

Zeal Okogeri

You Can Never

Go Wrong

By

<u>Being Kind</u>

A progeny of generations of African indigenous healers and mystics, Dr. Zeal Okogeri is a teacher in the fields of self-development and spiritual growth. Through his writings, teachings, and storytelling, he inspires love, kindness and compassion. He was born in Afikpo village, southeastern Nigeria. Zeal believes that if kindness is universally accepted and applied, everyone would benefit.

www.KindnessBooks.com

Meet our kindness story contributors

It is with great honor that I present the authors and story contributors in alphabetical order.

1. **Shannon Anderson** has taught for over 20 years, from first grade all the way up through the college level. She is also a presenter, a children's book author, a contributor to Highlights Magazine and Chicken Soup for the Soul, and the regional advisor for the Indiana Society for Children's Book Writers and Illustrators. Born and raised in Indiana, Shannon shares her home with her husband, Matt, and daughters, Emily and Maddie. To learn more or to contact her, you can visit her website at: www.shannonisteaching.com

2. **Mary Anglin-Coulter** graduated from Bellarmine University with a Bachelor of Arts degree, majoring in English and communication. After college, she worked in marketing, communication, and journalism and eventually as a paralegal. She currently owns her freelance writing and graphic design business. Her clients include Amazon.com, AllRecipes.com, Overstock.com, eBay.com, and many law firms in the United States and Canada. She has been published in Chicken Soup for the Soul, Small Town Living, The Outsiders Ally, The Ariel, Ripped Jeans and Bifocals, The Kentucky Standard, and ResCare Today. She can be reached at: mary@anglincoulter.com

3. **Ken Arlen** is a musician, saxophonist, band leader, and founder of Arlen Music Productions, a company based in the Chicago area that specializes in producing live music for special events. Past signature events include The Commander in Chief – Presidential Ball, NYE at the Bellagio Hotel in Las Vegas and numerous large-scale fundraisers, corporate events, and social events across North America. The story he contributed, "One Hardboiled Egg," was shared by his mother, Elizabeth Moore Arlen (born

in 1921), married to George Arlen (born in 1912), former CEO of Welby Clocks. There are three surviving children: Ken; Ken's older brother, Bob Arlen, a prominent estate attorney in Southern Florida; and his sister, Adrienne Duffy, founder of Big Futures, a company based in Edmonton, Canada that coaches and advises corporate clients and entrepreneurs. Ken can be reached at: www. arlenmusic.com

4. **Bernadette Fleming** lives in Huntington Beach, California with her husband, two children, and a cat. She is currently completing a doctorate degree in psychology. She has a master's degree in counseling and a bachelor's degree in psychology. Bernadette is a proud alumna of the University of Arizona. She loves working with children and adolescents. Bernadette is also a part-time fitness instructor. Her story has been published in Chicken Soup for the Soul books. You may contact Bernadette at: bduenas81@yahoo.com

5. **Melanie Hardy** is an attorney in Birmingham, Alabama. She lives with her husband and children. Her hobbies are writing, cooking, and working out. Her story has been published in Chicken Soup for the Soul books. She can be reached at: russymel@yahoo. Com

6. **Justin Horner** is a graphic designer living in Portland, Oregon. His story has been published in the New York Times, Reader's Digest, and other publications. He can be contacted via Facebook or www.justinwhorner.com

7. **Andreas Jones** is the founder of Combat Business Coaching, a leadership consultant. He is a former vice president at Sun Trust Bank, the bestselling author of Business Leader Combat, Business Strategist, and a contributor to Forbes, The Huffington Post, LifeHack.org, BizCatalyst360.com, and Army Combat Veteran. He works with business owners and business leaders to help them build high-performing businesses. Service in the U.S. Army forged Andreas's character. It tested his endurance, faith, and fortitude. He

217

describes it as "a trial by fire" and remains profoundly grateful for it. He can be reached at: www.CombatBusinessCoaching.com, www.Twitter.com/TheAndreasJones, www.AndreasHQ.com, or Facebook.

8. **Beverly Peace-Kayhill** is a retired university administrator. She is currently an image and career counselor and volunteers her time at Dress for Success, a non-profit organization that helps women prepare for job interviews. Beverly is writing her first novel, The Corn Garden. She has been a member of Toastmasters International, a public speaking organization, for 10 years. Originally from New York, Beverly now resides in Powder Springs, Georgia.

9. **Silana Lundin** earned a bachelor's degree in education and has served as a teacher, professional musician, and integrative health consultant. Over the past 25 years, she has facilitated numerous spiritual and personal growth workshops and book discussions for adults and youth. She's also been a guest speaker at events around the United States, sharing creative tools for spiritual growth and healing. Currently, Silana utilizes her skills in spiritual counseling to help those seeking to transcend blockages and live their highest purpose. Her greatest passion is being a student of life and serving others by living each day from the spirit of love and compassion. She can be reached at: silanalundin@gmail.com or www.ultimate-essentials.com

10. **Beverly MacKay** was born and raised in Boston, Massachusetts. After receiving her bachelor's degree in 1966 from Green Mountain College in Poultney, Vermont, she moved to Miami, Florida and began her lifelong career with Pan American World Airways as a flight attendant. When PANAM went out of business, she continued with Delta Airlines and retired in 2013 after serving for a total of 45 years as a flight attendant. She is currently a member of World Wings International, Inc., the philanthropic organization of

former Pan American World Airways, Inc. She is also a volunteer with United Service Organizations, which provides help to more than 10 million military service members and their families. In addition, she is a passionate supporter of animal charities. She lives in Smyrna, Georgia with her two kitties.

11. **Adrienne McCurdy** is an international consultant who designs and facilitates social change processes. She is motivated to support deeper levels of systems transformation through the development of both individuals and groups, leading her to co-found the University for the Third Horizon (H3Uni.org), RespectYouth.com, and research neighborhood hubs. Having lived, worked, studied, and travelled in more than 30 countries, Adrienne has developed an expertise in working across cultures, languages, and world views. Her background includes a Bachelor of Arts in social psychology; a Master of Science in Strategic Leadership toward Sustainability. Read her blog or explore possibilities for collaboration at: www. AdrienneMcCurdy.com.

12. **Jennifer Miguel** is an entrepreneur who is involved in her community, dedicating her time to helping others in need. She volunteers at a homeless shelter in Oahu, Hawaii as a job coach, helping individuals find employment. Her dream is to start a program that would provide school supplies for elementary school children and scholarships to college students whose parents are incarcerated. Jennifer can be contacted at: Miguel.jenn21@gmail. com or www.facebook.com/jennifer.miguel.18400

13. **Noelle Newell** is an interior designer and Allied Member of the American Society of Interior Designers (ASID). She creates interiors that are reflective of her client's personality and needs. Her approach to design is inspired by her travels, fine art, and nature. She loves to mix the new with the old. Perhaps it's a contemporary painting with an antique chest of drawers. After college, she studied

at the British Institute of Florence (art history) and The Sotheby's Institute of Art, London (decorative arts). Writing allows her to share her love of interior design with a wider audience. Noelle can be followed at @NoelleNewell1 on Twitter.

14. **Charles Onunkwo** was born and raised in Nigeria. He is currently the director of health information management at the Los Angeles County Department of Mental Health. He is also an adjunct professor of health science at East Los Angeles College, Monterey Park, California. He enjoys traveling and volunteers with a group of health care providers who visit Nigeria every year on Medical Mission, providing health education, promoting primary health care values, and giving free medicine to targeted vulnerable populations. He can be contacted through www.KindnessBooks.com

15. **Margie Pasero** lives in the Pacific Northwest on 12 beautiful acres. She enjoys eagles, elk, coyotes, bears, and an occasional cougar as well as salmon in her creek. She is a musician, playing alto sax in a swing band (consisting of mostly senior citizens) and clarinet in a community band. She's been married for 45 years and loves to read spiritual books, hike, travel, and knit. She is also a volunteer for senior services. She is a mother of two and a grandmother of six. Margie has had stories published in four Chicken Soup for the Soul books. Reach her at: heartbeats@nveture.com

16. **Stacey Shimabukuro** was born, raised, and spent nearly her entire life on the Hawaiian Islands, a place she happily calls her home. She was introduced to writing at the age of eight when her teacher instructed her to keep a journal, to free write, in an effort to overcome her shyness. In the fifth grade, she learned to write haiku (a traditional Japanese haiku is a three-line poem with 17 syllables, written in a 5/7/5 syllable count) and poetry. When some of her poetry was published in school newsletters, it awakened her to a possible innate talent she didn't know she possessed. Even though she takes an interest

in writing about subjects that encourage hope and kindness in the world, her main interest is animals. She's usually inspired by her pets, particularly her lop-eared bunny, Finn, who is always by her side whenever she is writing. She can be contacted at: stacey.shimabukuro@gmail.com

17. **Haylie Smart** holds a Bachelor of Arts in liberal arts and works as a seventh-grade English teacher in her hometown of Claremore, Oklahoma. She is currently writing her first novel under the pen name H.C. Smart. Her story was published in Chicken Soup for the Soul: The Power of Gratitude. She enjoys cooking, reading, journaling, and loving her nine nieces and nephews. She can be contacted at: haylie.smart@yahoo.com.

18. **Marlene Elvira Steinz** was born and raised in Stadl-Paura, Upper Austria, and is currently a lecturer of art history in Vienna, Austria. She has a master's degree in the history of art and a minor in archeology from the University of Vienna, as well as additional studies in philosophy and theology. She is also an integrative holistic energy worker, a world traveler, and a new mom of a two-year-old, Philomena Aurelia Sophie. She can be contacted via LinkedIn.

19. **Annmarie B. Tait** resides in Conshohocken, Pennsylvania with her husband, Joe Beck. Annmarie has had more than 50 stories published in various anthologies, including Chicken Soup for the Soul books, "Patchwork Path," the HCI "Ultimate" series and Reminisce magazine. In addition to writing, Annmarie enjoys singing and recording Irish and American folk music with her husband. You may contact her at: irishbloom@aol.com

20. **Takumi Tanabe** was born in a small town in Fukuoka Prefecture, in the northern part of Kyushu big island, Japan. For 30 years, he has worked as an English teacher and basketball coach for the boys' team at a private junior

high school in Kanagawa Prefecture, Japan, known as Keio Shonan-Fujisawa, which is a part of Keio University, one of the most prestigious universities in Japan. He earned his bachelor's degree in English from Waseda University in Tokyo, received a master's degree from the University of Michigan, and completed an advanced English language program at the University of Hawaii at Manoa, Honolulu. Takumi can be contacted through Facebook.

21. **Konchog Tobden** is a Tibetan Buddhist monk, born and raised in a small rural village in southern India. At age 13, he joined the Ayang Rinpoche's Monastery/Drikung Kagyu Monastery in Bylakuppe, south India, where he studied general subjects such as mathematics, reading and writing, and English and Buddhist ritual prayers. In 1991 he was admitted to the philosophy school, where he studied fundamental Buddhist scriptures and Buddhist philosophy for 13 years, graduating in 2006. In 2007, he became responsible for the monastic discipline of Ayang Rinpoche's Monastery. Thereafter, he served as the Abbot of the Kagyu Monastic Institute. He is currently completing his master's degree in Buddhism at the Centre of Buddhist Studies – The University of Hong Kong in Hong Kong. He can be contacted at: kon_topden@yahoo.com or through Facebook.

22. **John Villemonte** was born in Madison, Wisconsin. He earned a bachelor's degree in music from Skidmore College in Saratoga Springs, New York. At a young age, his father, James Villemonte, a professor of civil engineering, accepted an assignment in Calcutta, India, and his entire family lived there for three years. This period abroad inspired John to discover his appreciation for diversity, love for travel, and passion for music (piano, guitar, and songwriting). John has since recorded nine albums of his own original music. He is also devoted to spiritual studies and developed a "big-picture" point of view. He looks for truth by studying patterns. Follow the

patterns, he believes, and they will reveal many truths about life. An avid nature photographer, he enjoys traveling the country with his wife, Muriel, and recording their journeys as they go. John lives with his wife, Muriel, in Chanhassen, Minnesota, where he works as a web designer. He can be reached at: villemonte@gmail.com

23. **Brenda Watterson** loves to read, write, and spend time with her family. Her work, both fiction and non-fiction have appeared in various anthologies including Chicken Soup for the Soul books, Listen to Your Mother and WOW Women on Writing. She is currently working on her first novel. Brenda lives in Algonquin, Illinois with her husband and children. She can be reached at brendah2oson@gmail.com

24. **Ferida Wolff** has 17 published children's books and three essay books for adults. She is also a frequent contributor to the Chicken Soup for the Soul books, writes poetry, and practices meditation. She can be reached at: feridawolff@msn.com

25. **Zhang Yue** was born and raised in Tianjin, China. She graduated from the University of Tianjin with a bachelor's degree in finance and economics. She currently works for an international trade firm and lives in Tianjin, China. She can be contacted through www.KindnessBooks.com

Thank you to each one of you for being a part of this uplifting book.

With much Love,

Dr. Zeal Okogeri
Island of Oahu, Hawaii
www.KindnessBooks.com

Give a copy of this book as a gift to someone special. It is a wonderful present for most occasions.

- Weddings
- Anniversaries
- Birthdays – parents, siblings, children, grandparents, friends
- Births
- Graduations
- Holidays – tokens of affection on Valentine's Day
- Easter
- Mother's Day
- Father's Day
- Christmas
- Just because – a special occasion
- Donate copies to humanitarian organizations & libraries
- Fundraising
- Great gift for students, teachers, professors, managers, spiritual leaders, social workers, healthcare providers, law enforcement officials, and government officials.

For information on how to place large-volume orders, please visit our website: www.Kindnessbooks.com

Dr. Zeal Okogeri travels and speaks worldwide.
For more information, please visit www.Kindnessbooks.com

Permissions

A Random Act of Roadside Assistance. Reprinted by permission of Justin Horner.

Kindness Soften Our Hearts. Reprinted by permission of Zeal Okogeri, from his book, Relentless Generosities of Spirit. 2014.

Elementary School Student Bails His Teacher Out of Prison. Reprinted by permission of Zeal Okogeri, from his book, Relentless Generosities of Spirit. 2014.

The War Intensified. Reprinted by permission of Zeal Okogeri, from his book, Journey To Freedom. 2012.

My Family's Refugee Story. Reprinted by permission of Zeal Okogeri, from his book, Journey To Freedom. 2012.

The War Ends. Reprinted by permission of Zeal Okogeri, from his book, Journey To Freedom. 2012.

My First Plane Ride. Reprinted by permission of Zeal Okogeri, from his book, Relentless Generosities of Spirit 2014.

The Gift of Letting Go. Reprinted by permission of Zeal Okogeri, from his book, Relentless Generosities of Spirit. 2014.

Be Willing to Ask for Help. Reprinted by permission of Zeal Okogeri, from his book, Relentless Generosities of Spirit. 2014.

Be True to Yourself. Reprinted by permission of Zeal Okogeri, from his book, Relentless Generosities of Spirit. 2014.

Be Calm. Reprinted by permission of Zeal Okogeri, from his book, Relentless Generosities of Spirit. 2014.

Permissions

Learning to Let Go. Reprinted by permission of Zeal Okogeri, from his book, Relentless Generosities of Spirit. 2014.

The Richest Man in the World. Reprinted by permission of Zeal Okogeri, from his book, Relentless Generosities of Spirit. 2014.

Lover of All Life. Reprinted by permission of Zeal Okogeri, from his book, Relentless Generosities of Spirit. 2014.

Every Act of Love Makes a Difference. Reprinted by permission of Zeal Okogeri, from his book, Relentless Generosities of Spirit. 2014.

Follow Your Heart. Reprinted by permission of Zeal Okogeri, from his book, Relentless Generosities of Spirit. 2014.

Be Willing to Ask for Help. Reprinted by permission of Zeal Okogeri, from his book, Relentless Generosities of Spirit. 2014.

If You Don't Take Care of Body, where do You Plan to Live? Reprinted by permission of Zeal Okogeri, from his book, Relentless Generosities of Spirit. 2014.

Being Honest is Kindness. Reprinted by permission of Zeal Okogeri, from his book, Relentless Generosities of Spirit 2014.

Watch Out for Distractions. Reprinted by permission of Zeal Okogeri, from his book, Relentless Generosities of Spirit 2014.

Sources

Forsyth, Frederick. *The Biafra Story: The Making of an African Legend.* Pen & Sword Military 2019.

Okogeri, Zeal. *Relentless Generosities of Spirit.* Light Books Publishing, November 2014.

For more information on Dr. Zeal Okogeri's speaking and travel schedule, pease visit: www.Kindnessbooks.com or visit his Facebook page.

Made in the USA
Monee, IL
04 May 2024

57976034R00134